Playing for England

John Hemmingham

peakpublish

Peakpublish
An imprint of Peak Platform
New Bridge
Calver
Hope Valley
S32 3XT

First published by Peakpublish 2010

Printed in England

A CIP catalogue record for this book is available from the
British Library

ISBN: 978-1-907219-10-8 (Hbk)

www.peakplatform.com

Chapter One

"There's fifteen of you here. Some of you will drop out next week, some the week after, but some will be determined enough to come back having learned two notes and that will be good. I'm looking for those who can do that and they'll be the ones who get to join the band, the others will fade away. Nobody will be able to get five notes." Said Clive Hawley, Band Leader of the 150th Wadsley Church Scout Band, Sheffield.

It was some time in 1970 and I was seven years old and a member of the Cub Scouts in Sheffield. I heeded the words of the Band Leader but two notes were no good for me. I knew that if you're any good on the bugle you can play five notes, not two. As with so many things that now make sense I found out that I wasn't one to shirk a challenge. I was going to make sure I could play five notes by the next week. Following a psychological profiling almost 40 years later I learned that the best way to get me to do something is tell me that I can't do it!

1

After seven days of practicing, driving the family and neighbours mad inside and outside our house, (particularly on the back step pointing down the garden due to the echo that came back) I could play five notes which I knew would put me in the group of bugle players known as the firsts. I liked that, 'the firsts,' sounded good. I also knew that Clive Hawley lived a stone's throw away and was good friends with my next door neighbour so some of the practicing was directed straight at his house. Little wonder then that when I reported back to the next week's practice he already knew that I could play the five notes required to make the firsts and in I went, joining the band at seven.

That wasn't what I regarded as the best achievement of my very short life so far, because we'd also won the cup at football that year - which was the best experience ever. Well, to be honest we shared the cup with St. Polycarps Cubs because we drew after full time and extra time and we drew again 5-5 on penalties, so the powers that be decided to give each side the cup for 6 months each. Some final! Although we didn't know it at the time, the team we played, St. Polycarps, were the foundation side for what was and still is a very well known Sheffield Sunday team, Sheffield Rangers FC. I was to play for them a few years later.

Why was it so exciting to win the cup at football? Quite simply because I am totally football mad. The game was played in Hillsborough Park which is next to Sheffield Wednesday's ground. I could see the ground from my bedroom window, even the electronic scoreboard which was the first of its kind in the country, and I was going to play there one day, no doubt at all. So to win my first medal right next to the Sheffield Wednesday ground was as good as it gets for a seven year old.

This fantasy land I had created for myself must have had an influence on my decision, at eight years old, to pack in all school work. I did this in a most logical way having worked out that I didn't need to do it because I was going to be a footballer and was happy to explain this to my class teacher and parents. I couldn't understand what all the fuss was about but ended up in front of the headmaster explaining the same thing that I had already done to everyone else. Credit due to Mr Ellingham, headmaster at Marlcliffe County Junior School, who managed to get straight on to my wave length and logic by explaining how goal average was worked out and how the league tables worked and that the papers carried match reports in them that may have some difficult words in if I didn't learn to read in English lessons. I left the headmaster's office completely convinced that to be a footballer I would have to pay attention in maths and English or it was not going to work. Little surprise then that my best subjects ended up being maths and English, another thing that I didn't realise until now. The English part of things does help when you have to write a book some forty years later, I might add.

The old adage, 'show me the boy at seven and I'll show you the man,' could certainly have been applied to me at that age but who would have known what was going to happen twenty-three years later, nobody I'm sure.

I continued to become more-and-more obsessed with football, maths and English along with all my friends. Only friends who were into football could be in our gang, which was made up of the five best players in our class. We would play football in the school yard from before 8 a.m. in the morning until 9 a.m. when we had to go into lessons. We would carry on at 10.30 a.m. for fifteen minutes at morning break and an hour at lunch and fifteen minutes for afternoon break and then the total score would be totted up for the day and the result announced to all.

Needless-to-say, football dominated everything that I did from that early age. In the early 70's a very memorable event took place at Hillsborough. Santos, Pele's side from Brazil, came to play Sheffield Wednesday in a friendly game. Brazil were the World Cup holders having won in Mexico and this was massive. Now for some reason this game was played on a weekday afternoon when we were all supposed to be at school. The lucky ones had got permission from their parents to have the day off and were being taken to the game, which commanded a 55,000 attendance. The rest of us were stuck at school and not very happy. We could see and hear the crowd from the school playground and it was too much. A sit down protest seemed to be the only reasonable course of action and I was always going to be the one to organise that kind of thing. It was not to be unruly at all but because in the same pragmatic way that I had decided I didn't need to study a few years earlier I

4

had figured the situation out and decided that it simply wasn't fair that some kids were allowed to go to the game and others weren't. I was right of course but hadn't really thought it through. The game was about to kick off and they were hardly going to say, "Alright kids, off you go". I had managed to rally considerable support for the cause and long after we should have been back in school following afternoon break we were camped in the rounders bowler's square painted on the tarmac of our playground singing, 'We shall not be moved'. That was until Mr Thraves, the much feared deputy head, came out threatening us with the slipper unless we got back inside immediately and behaved ourselves. The ring leader, me, was summonsed to see Mr Thraves and I feared the worst but somehow must have been able to talk my way out of it. Importantly for me, it would have been done via an absolute belief that I was right and could put the case across in such a way that teachers understood that I just couldn't help it, it was what I believed and not mischievous or deliberately disruptive.

Mr Thraves and Mr Reaney, were the two teachers who accompanied us to the final of the Sanderson Trophy whilst in our final year at junior school. My Dad used to watch us when he could and his speciality was encouragement from the touch line. This encouragement from the touchline thing must run in the family. One of my team mates once asked me, in a not very complimentary way, who was the bloke on the touchline who kept shouting, to which I had to reply, "Oh, er... that's my Dad." He, of course, claims that he won several matches for us, even to this day, who knows?

We were a good team. I can't remember ever losing a game, beating all the schools we played in the Sheffield area and winning the final, 4-2. It didn't get better than that at ten years of age, we even had the South Yorkshire Times come and take a photo of us in the playground and Alan Thompson, Sheffield Wednesday's centre half, came to the school to present us with our medals.

It was also around this time, that another major event in my life took place, which was to further cement my allegiance to Sheffield Wednesday, if that were possible. My mother had many talents and amongst other things was a dressmaker and she had somehow got the order to make the wedding dress for the daughter of Derek Dooley. Derek Dooley, for anyone who doesn't know, remains to this day Sheffield Wednesday's record goal scorer with 46 goals in one season. Sadly, now passed away, Derek was the manager of Sheffield Wednesday at the time and he was coming to the house to see his daughter's dress. This prompted the dressing up of the house, particularly the staircase that he would walk up, with Sheffield Wednesday scarves, of which I had six. It was a time when you wore scarves around your neck, one on each wrist and two tied to your belt loops dangling down each leg. My autograph book was positioned on the bottom step with a big sign saying, "Sign here please Mr Dooley." Derek arrived with Silvia, his wife, and their daughter and of course was immediately accosted by me and instructed to sign the autograph book and to be escorted to my bedroom to see the masses of Wednesday photos, scarves, programmes and other memorabilia that I had collected and still have today. "You run up first and I'll be with you soon," he said. I was unaware that Derek

6

had tragically lost his leg to gangrene following a break playing for Wednesday against Preston. Derek came upstairs to look at my bedroom nonetheless and even got Tommy Craig, our record signing at £100,000 and a record at the time for a teenager, to drop a signed team photo in a few days later as an additional surprise.

Derek did go on to become chairman of Sheffield United following a particularly badly timed Christmas Eve sacking as manager of Wednesday and has a major road named after him in Sheffield, namely, Derek Dooley Way. My Dooley experience has stayed with me for life and I am not alone when I say I can't praise or thank him enough for that.

Mentioning Sheffield United is painful except when in the same sentence as, Boxing Day massacre 4-0, 1979, Steel City Semi Final at Wembley 2-1, 1993 (should have been 10-1) and any other of our famous victories. I have to say that my Dad is a Sheffield United supporter and took me to see them when Best, Charlton and Law came to town. Their ground was rubbish, it only had three sides because it was a cricket pitch too and thankfully, that wasn't for me. Thank God then for Jonathan Whitley, my next door neighbour, who not only trained me, (he was a few years older and played for Sheffield Boys and later Matlock Town, so he was qualified) but for taking me to Hillsborough on numerous occasions before I was old enough to go with my friends. Heaven forbid I had become a Unitedite. No, that was never going to happen, never!

Growing up in Hillsborough was great as a kid, but very different at the same time. It is dominated by the football club and when I was a kid other institutions too, such as the local mental hospital, Middlewood Hospital. This meant that it was quite normal to have those patients that weren't any harm to the public walking our street every day. As a kid this was a great source of amusement as we would interact regularly with patients that would sing us songs, give us buns and could easily be persuaded to do any number of other things at the drop-of-a-hat. It was normal for us to see men in white coats running down the road in the middle of the night chasing an escapee with the van behind them ready to pick them up. I'm sure this had an influence on how crazy we have ended up as a group, as the hard core of band members grew up in this environment and we're all a little mad. The other thing we did as kids was play football all day, everyday, during school holidays and weekends from dawn until dusk. Couple this with bugle playing and a good sense of humour and you get us as the end product.

A typical day then would see me wake up in the bedroom with no central heating, (I did get pneumonia when I was 5 years old) scrape the ice off the window and look out onto Hillsborough. I'd then get ready to go to school, with my football kit on under my normal clothes - why, I don't know - have lessons in between football, leave school, encounter a few 'patients' from the mental hospital en route to my paper round. For some reason, probably the taste, I would take a tin opener from the cutlery draw at home with a desert spoon, pop them in my Wrangler denim jacket top pocket (with Wednesday patches all over it) and buy and eat a tin of

Ambrosia Creamed Rice before my paper round. We all had denim jackets at that time, not all had patches and I still have the very jacket in a box in the loft to this day. Albeit far too small, it couldn't be thrown away. After the paper round, I'd spend more money in the paper shop on sweets than I had earned and then go home. We would then roam the streets, not usually causing trouble but there was the odd occasion when our football went through a house window, and we did play knock and run. We also had a bucket with a piece of string attached that we filled with water, then tied the string to a tree next to the kerb and trail the string across the footpath and over the garden wall of the nearest house. We then waited for a poor, unsuspecting person to walk over the string and then pulled it so that the bucket of water poured over them. They would then usually chase us, which was all good training I suppose.

At weekends we would play football all day when we weren't at 'the match.' 'The match' was a Wednesday home game or, on alternate Saturdays, the Wednesday reserves. The admission fee to these games was greatly reduced and therefore kid friendly and hundreds of us used to go. Our obsession with football was such that on Sundays we would play a game in the Wednesday training ground car park in the morning, have Sunday dinner and go straight to Hillsborough Park for the big game, that seemed to be up to 15 a side, kicked off at about 2.30 p.m. and finished at dusk, when the park keeper threw us out. We would then probably verbally abuse him and get chased out of the park and then have to be on our guard the next time we went to the park because surprise, surprise, he didn't forget, nor should he have with hindsight .

I started watching Wednesday when we were on our way to the worst period on the club's history known as the 'dark years'. This was the period when the local newspaper in Sheffield, The Star, launched their 'Save Our Owls' campaign which was designed to rally support that would fend off relegation to the 3rd Division for the first time in their history. I remember going away to York City for a night game and holding up the 'Save Our Owls' banner with pride for The Star photographer as he took our photo for the next day's paper. If my memory serves me right we survived the season when, on the last day, we beat Bolton Wanderers at Hillsborough with a goal by Ken Knighton to make it 2-1 to The Owls. Ken Knighton became a hero but the sting in the tail was that Wednesday were relegated the next season to Division 3 for the first time ever and almost to Division 4 the next season. A win on the last day of the season against Southend United sent them down instead of us. That game saw my first participation in a pitch invasion but it was a celebration of thousands of fans deliriously happy that we hadn't got relegated again!

It was about this time that I started to progress to going to the games on my own, aged eleven. When I say on my own I mean without an adult. This included away games on the train and it makes me smile to think what people would say now about a group of eleven year olds going to a night game, away at Chesterfield, on the train and at the height of football hooliganism too! Clearly my mates and I survived and learned a few things on the way that would help us throughout our football watching lives. In particular, the ability to sense the potential for trouble or a problem about to happen which I'm sure most football supporters are familiar with, serves me very well to this day. It was actually no more prevalent in Chesterfield than in the Sheffield train or bus stations when you returned from an away game. Invariably Sheffield United fans would be waiting somewhere for stragglers or the first Wednesday fans back before the main body returned, so, you learned to be amongst the main body of fans and all was well.

My football watching was funded by various young entrepreneurial ventures, such as car washing and a great paper round taking in Carlton Road and Hillsborough School, bang opposite Sheffield Wednesday. The first delivery was to Beres Pork Shop with Mr Beres, an imposing figure who I think was of Polish or Hungarian origin, who would give a knowing nod and wink each day. Everyone in Sheffield knows of Beres pork sandwiches; simply the best, is a very fitting phrase. Ironically, they have just been introduced in the refreshment bars on the terraces at Hillsborough, eight years after I first campaigned to get them there (not being one to blow my own trumpet you understand). The best paid part-time job I had was at the Kentucky Fried Chicken shop making boxes and later progressing and then cooking the chicken. At that time I was on more money part time than I was in my first job which meant funding away games wasn't a problem.

I had a parallel life going on at the same time as my football life. That life was one of piano lessons on Dixon

11

Road and yes, you guessed it, a stone's throw from Hillsborough Stadium and I was also a member of the Wadsley Scout Band, entering competitions all over the country and often marching around the district hoping that none of my mates would be out watching as that would be a disaster. I did get an awful lot of stick from my mates for my musical activities and there were times when I could easily have run off to play football instead of taking the piano lessons but as usual my parents were right when they said that I'd appreciate it later in life and I do. Mrs Marrison was my piano teacher. She and her husband were lovely people and often, if I was early for my lesson, Mrs Marrison would say, "Nip in the back and talk to Mr Marrison for a while". They were season ticket holders in the South Stand and we used to talk anything and everything Sheffield Wednesday in that mutually appreciative way that only genuine football fans can do.

One incredible set of games that I talked about with Mr & Mrs Marrison and in fact the whole country were talking about, was the 3rd round FA Cup games between Wednesday and Arsenal in 1978. Jack Charlton was manager and we were in the third division. As usual, Arsenal, who you just can't like if you are a Wednesday fan, were riding high in the top flight of English football. In the days before the game at Hillsborough it had snowed heavily and fans were asked to turn up at the ground on the Friday to clear the pitch so that the game could go ahead. No need to ask twice. I went down with my school mate, John Pearson, who, although we didn't know it at the time, would later play for Wednesday. About sixty or so fans were there in the morning with shovels, wheel barrows and bags of enthusiasm including us. Disappointingly we got the job of clearing the terraces on the Kop. We wanted to be on the pitch but at fifteen you can't really argue so on we soldiered. Slowly the weather took it's toll on most of the volunteers until there were only six of us left. We saw a figure walking towards us from the tunnel and to our surprise it was Bert McGee, the chairman at the time who had walked around the pitch from the tunnel carrying a tray with six mugs of tea, for us. What a great gesture.

We played Arsenal the next day and drew 1-1, and then went to Highbury for the replay and drew again 1-1. Amazing results considering the difference in league position but what was to come made this tie unique in English FA Cup history. In those days after two drawn games teams played each other at a neutral ground to settle the tie. We played at Filbert Street, home of Leicester City and drew again 2-2 which meant we had a fourth game the next week and drew again 3-3. You cannot believe the excitement we felt at these games when we had only known relegation previously. Finally we played a fifth game and lost 2-0 which has become a typical Arsenal result when playing us throughout my life but the legend of the Marathon Men was born as was the longest running FA Cup tie in English football. We were at all the Leicester games thanks to John's Dad, Gerry, who took us there in his light blue Capri, happy days.

Happy days indeed but nothing beats the best Wednesday match ever. The Boxing Day massacre which to the uninitiated was Sheffield Wednesday beating Sheffield United at Hillsborough, Boxing Day 1979, 11 a.m. kick-off to avoid crowd trouble. They were top, we were third in the then third division and almost 50,000 fans turned out to see the game, still a record. Wednesday won 4-0, yes, 4-0, and you cannot begin to imagine how happy that made me and thousands of others that day. You couldn't find a United fan anywhere after the game, they were all in hiding. We phoned up, called at houses but couldn't find one anywhere, such was the humiliation.

That episode of my Wednesday supporting did nothing but cement what was already an obsession and my mates and I followed Wednesday the length and breadth of the country, with very little success, other than the odd promotion, followed by relegation and some good cup runs. This included a semi-final that I watched at Highbury, with a broken leg, a footballing accident playing for The Admiral Rodney, our local Sunday League team. During my youth I simultaneously developed a passion for England and the England football team. I watched the team go out to Poland in 1973 with Tomachevski (the clown) in goal, performing heroics and shared the disappointment with the nation, aged 10. I went on the school trip to Wembley to see Cruyff and co. play for Holland against England and again to see England v Argentina but can't remember any of their players. I still have a scarf that I bought for 55p showing the England team in the home internationals 1973/74 and take it to all the games. It's usually dangling from my trumpet (you can't say that every day).

These Wembley appearances, of course, had a lasting impression and I went back to Wembley for the England v Scotland match, the one after they invaded the pitch and broke the goal posts. I had to move away from Sheffield in 1980, when my Dad changed his job which was a big shock, not because of what I found in Marlow where we moved to, but because my parents had always said they would never move. I understood that to literally mean, we would never move, so there was the shock, I ended up in Marlow, in Buckinghamshire, doing two years of A' levels in one year at High Wycombe College. This made it more difficult to get to games because of the distance and cost but I had passed my driving test and inherited my Mum's 1967 Escort, so I had wheels. These wheels next changed to an Escort van, that was relatively new in comparison, so I got to more matches. I particularly remember Portsmouth away when it absolutely threw it down and I mean threw it down. The football special train, 'Inter City Owl' was delayed a few hours on the way down and back due to flooding and problems on the line caused by the excessive rain. Fortunately, by a fluke, I managed to get a seat in the covered stand, by mistakenly queuing up at the wrong turnstile. The rest of the Wednesday fans were cold and soaked to the skin on the open terrace that was the away end and we lost, not so happy days.

My Mum seemed to settle into life 'down south', even developing two distinct accents for telephone callers depending where they were ringing from. If you know Hyacinth Bouquet you're not far off. It was quite comical when the phone rang; my Mum would answer it in the posh voice, edging her bets and then slip immediately back into broad Sheffield if the call came from 'up north'. Something like.........ring ring, 'Marlow 72305, Oh, ello luv, you alright?' to which there would be an echo around the house from me, my brother Chris and my Dad, 'Oh, oh, oh, ello luv', times three. It was also the time of the Chas and Dave hit, 'Rabbit', so whenever my Mum was nagging us, which would be everyday, the three of us would sing from wherever we were in the house, 'Rabbit, Rabbit, Rabbit, Rabbit, Rabbit'. We thought it was funny, she didn't. If the truth be known I didn't really get on with my Mum, maybe she expected a bit too much from me and I couldn't live up to the standards but for many years we would row seemingly almost continuously. Looking back, the things she used to go on about have benefited me now but at the time it made for a miserable existence. I'm sure she meant well.

My brother wasn't into football at all, not in the slightest. He was more mechanically minded and long before he got into building motor bikes and cars he dismantled anything and everything in the house, including any radios, tape recorders, stereos, walkie talkies, transformers, you name it and he would never put them back together. These things could also include items that belonged to anyone else in the house so I had to keep my little match radio close, or hidden, if I wanted it to stay in one piece. He had been taken to matches by my Dad but insisted on taking his Marvel comics with him and would read them throughout the whole game. Mind you, it was Sheffield United, so who can blame him?

Chris was five years older than me which did have its advantages in certain areas such as his bookshelf that included not very well hidden, 'dirty books', that I could read and put back without any blame. It was very funny when my Mum found them, incredibly funny when you're thirteen. She also found his air-rifle repeater hidden between his mattress and bed, as if she wouldn't when she changed the beds? The same gun had shot me up the arse previously in the hands of my brother, who swore blind he'd shot all twenty eight pellets that the gun held, as he pointed it at my eye. I told him he hadn't and he decided to point it at my arse to test it. I was right and the pellet went through my trousers and pants and lodged itself in my right buttock. I can still feel it now. Well, we were in the garden at the time and he ran up the garden, up the back steps, shot up the stairs and locked himself in his bedroom to be followed by me all at lightening pace. Although I was five years younger than him I was the same size and started to smash his door down, I was going to kill him. We would fight most days given the chance and had done from an early age, great training for school where I didn't have any trouble with fighting. He realised that I was really going to knock the door down and kill him so started to barter through the door. The outcome being that a deal was struck which involved me not killing him, fifty pence (which was a lot of money then!) and a look at his Swedish 'dirty book'. This book wasn't on the shelf because my Mum really would have gone berserk at what was in there. I had to not tell my Mum or Dad which I didn't and can remember going away to Scotland in our caravan at the end of that week and lying in the bunk bed picking at the pellet lodged in my arse until it finally came out, it was flat which demonstrates how hard it hit me.

The only time he got interested in my football was when he asked me to play in a game for the Marlow venture scouts. I followed in his footsteps to Wadsley

Church Cubs years earlier and he had carried on and joined the Marlow venture scouts when the family moved south. He knew I wasn't bad at football so was quite pleased when it turned out I was better than those we were playing against and he could be proud of his little brother, who was actually about six inches bigger than him by now.

Sadly, both my Mum and brother died within three weeks of each other in June/July 2001, my annus horribilis My brother had been diagnosed with a brain tumour when he was twenty nine and had operations and treatment of varying kinds for fourteen years, leading to recovery on a few occasions but the cancer finally got him and he died aged forty-three leaving a daughter, Hannah, and son, James. About eighteen months before my brother's death my Mum, who along with my Dad, had continually looked after my brother during his illness, was diagnosed with bowel cancer. My Mum went to my brother's funeral in an ambulance and saw through the proceedings on a stretcher at the front of the crematorium. We all knew it wouldn't be long until we returned for my Mum's funeral and so it was, three weeks later.

There are a couple of things that this kind of experience does drive home, one, that despite the fact that they have always been there, people really aren't around forever. The other being that the motto, 'live for today' and 'don't put off till tomorrow something that you can do today', does have a lot going for it. It certainly brought it home to me in a big way. I do know that my Mum and Chris were both quite proud of the fact that I'd started 'the band' and achieved a certain amount of notoriety even if they didn't really understand or get it in any way.

The band? Did I not mention it? Read on......................

Chapter Two

So, for some reason in the 1990s I decided to relive my youth and buy myself a bugle, just like the one that I'd learnt to play all those years earlier in the Cub Scouts. I can't remember where I bought it from but remember that it arrived in a cardboard box, properly wrapped and even having tape around most of the instrument to protect it.

At the time I was a member of the Rivelin Owls who travelled to many Sheffield Wednesday games on a coach from the Stannington area of Sheffield and was run by my old mate, Lou Wilson. One such game was one of Wednesday's finest, the League Cup Final v Manchester United at Wembley in 1991. We'd managed to get tickets in the Olympic gallery which sort of hung from the roof of the old Wembley Stadium above the fans. This being a once in a lifetime experience, or so we thought at the time, about fifty of us booked into a London hotel for the weekend.

You cannot imagine the excitement on that coach - we Wednesday fans going to a final, many of us for the first time, and to add to it all I'd taken my bugle and played it most of the way down. Some of the lads inspired by this went to the market on Portabella Road on the morning of the game and bought four bugles, one each.

On entering the stadium they were waving their bugles about and blowing merrily with varying success and my bugle was up my jumper. This was supposed to be the posh area of the stadium and it didn't take long before the stewards had confiscated four bugles but I'd managed to keep mine hidden, as, being a Yorkshireman and having paid good money for it, I wasn't going to lose it.

We won the game 1-0, with the legend that is John Sheridan scoring the only goal of the game, and a Manchester United side against whom few gave us a chance, as we were a division below them at the time. The celebrations afterwards were second-to-none, inevitably involving the bugle being blown all the way home and in the Holly Bush pub when we got back.

The bugle had made it to Wembley but not made it's debut. We were to go to Wembley again five times in 1993 when every Wednesday supporter was skint. As a domestic football fan you couldn't have attended more games in a season than Wednesday fans did that year. We reached the FA Cup Final and lost after a replay again at Wembley to Arsenal. Remember the Marathon Men of 1978? Now you know why I don't like Arsenal, good team as they were and still are, they could have let us win one. Clearly we wanted to win at least one Cup but the really important game of that season came at Wembley in the semi final of the FA Cup and for one reason only - we played Sheffield United.

The bugle again made it to Wembley but was left in the coach as we were in normal seats and the worst thing that could happen was that I'd get it confiscated on entering the ground and get refused entry. This was far too big a gamble to take, nobody from Sheffield wanted to miss the Steel City Derby to beat all Derbies. Wednesday battered United that day and the chant of, 'it should have been 10-1,' was very fitting and it would have been but for Alan Kelly, United goalkeeper, who performed heroics that day. Remarkably the game went to extra time but Wednesday scored to win the game 2-1, absolutely fantastic, history made.

We made it back to the coach in Wembley car park and somehow managed to take the skylight off the rear roof opening, then, standing on the seats and looking like a tank commander from the outside, I popped out just in time to play the death march to six Unitedites carrying their big flag like pall bearers would carry a coffin. They took it well, not that they had much choice carrying a flag of that size and surrounded by ecstatic Wednesdayites.

It was later that year that the bugle really came to fame. Another Rivelin Owls trip took us to Everton for a night match and I'd managed to smuggle the bugle into Goodison Park and the rest of the lads knew it was up my jumper. Eighty minutes had gone and we were winning 2-0 with goals by Mark Bright and a looping header from the edge of the box by Carlton Palmer. This was indeed a rare event and whether or not this was the inspiration, I was encouraged by the lads to take the bugle out from up my jumper and play the fanfare to Ida. This was the tune that Wednesday fans always sing when we score, having a distinct fanfare at the beginning followed by everyone joining in and it went down a storm. 'Do it again, do it again!' so I obliged and the massive following that day joined in again and again.

Later that night I was back at home, in Stocksbridge (just north of Sheffield) at the time, listening to the late-night phone-in show on the local radio station when they asked if anyone knew who had scored the goals in the Everton v Wednesday game. I phoned them up and said I don't want to go on air but it was Bright and Palmer and by the way I was the bugler in the crowd. I'd taken the bugle to a few other games and there had been a bit of a campaign in the local sports paper, The Green Un, to find the mystery bugler. The DJ said he was going to put me on air to say what I'd told him, so I did.

Unbeknown to me, Trevor Francis, the Sheffield Wednesday manager at the time and his son were sat at home listening to the show. Trevor rang the show and asked if he could have my number. They rang me to ask if it was alright to pass on my number. Imagine, God asks for your number and the bloke thinks I'm not going to give it to him! I went to bed wondering when the phone would ring and of course it was whilst I was in the bath the next day that it did. My girlfriend at the time passed me the phone and Trevor said he thought it was fantastic what I'd done the night before at Everton and that when he had played in Italy the teams would have drums banging and they created a great atmosphere that would inspire their teams. He asked if I had any mates that would bang a drum. I told him that I didn't know but would certainly ask them.

Shortly after that phone call from God, God's Dad phoned up and I was still in the bath. God's Dad was Sheffield Wednesday Chairman, Dave Richards, later to become Sir Dave Richards and now Chairman of the Premier League. Dave said that he'd had a chat with Trevor who was keen to get something going and offered to fund the purchase of some drums. I already knew, from my scout band days, that the best drums to have would be tenor drums and Premier Drums at that. I agreed to get back to him after I'd had a word with my mates as I'd said earlier to Trevor.

There was a considerable group of us who had season tickets on the Kop, so I began to ask around to see if anyone was interested in forming a band. The drums were bought and the band was born. There were six of us who made our debut on the Hillsborough Kop for the first game. Along with myself there was Murray (Stephen Holmes), my mate from school, Loz (Laurence Garratty) who was a member of the Sanderson Trophy winning team in 1975, Craig Zelly, Michael Denton and his mate, Ian. What a ramshackle it was really, looking back but we were nothing if not keen. I had spent the best part of the day prior to the game teaching two of them to play trumpets and the others who had never hit a drum before were banging away to find that after a while, if you don't protect your hands, you get blisters that bleed. You see, when you're as obsessed as we are and your club calls, you answer the call with everything you've got.

We found our place on the Kop and went for it big time. It must have sounded horrific but we stuck at it and the fans joined in creating a great atmosphere both home and away. You see, what it sounds like doesn't really matter, to a certain extent anyway, it's more about timing and volume with a tune. We coined the phrase that, 'The man on the terrace is not Pavarotti nor are we the Halle Orchestra!' This sums up the concept of the band very well, even to this day.

Don't, please, mistake this for some sort of none-caring attitude because the truth is far from that, very far. We care passionately about what we do which is creating an atmosphere at football grounds that inspires a better performance from the players on the pitch. It is a well known fact that increased volume of support works as inspiration to teams and we orchestrate that support.

From the very start we have all naturally put everything we have into our playing and fortunately we have a knack of knowing what to do and when, which is so important when it comes to getting the respect of other fans. We are just like the fan with the biggest mouth who normally starts a chant at other grounds but we have a bigger mouth and yes, we do get it wrong sometimes but manage to laugh about it and start something else up, usually the chant we knew we should have been doing in the first place.

Then I was contacted by the press for the first time. The local press had run a story on, 'who's the mystery bugler?' and then they wrote an article to reveal who it was. That was when we learned that when you've been in the paper, and the radio and TV stations pick up on the stories, you're on air the next day. So it was that my first national interview was with John Inverdale, on Radio 5 and I remember being extremely nervous. Until then I'd only sold trucks so I was a confident sort but not national radio confident. From what I can remember the interview went well and local TV followed. It was a good fun story and we were enjoying the experience.

Not all comments were good and that's still the case, we have those who love what we do and those who don't. One of the biggest disappointments was that the Wednesday supporter (or two of them) who wrote the weekly fans view in the 'Green Un' wrote some not very complimentary stuff about us and we felt that they should be on the side of anyone who was genuinely trying to help the team win. This wasn't the case and although we can't understand those who want to go to a football match and be quiet.

The media interest in us continued to grow as we went around the country supporting Wednesday at various top grounds. We would have been there anyway as we had been for the previous fifteen to twenty years but obviously when you're drowning out the opposition you get noticed a bit more. When I say we, the early years saw myself and Murray, who had established himself as the main drummer, attend all the home and away games with more joining us at home games and some away.

The media soon caught up with us again thanks to an up and coming, Wednesday supporting, TV producer who worked for Sky's, 'Soccer AM'. We got the call to go on to the programme that was, and still is, the football culture show. I didn't realise that at the time being an advent of ordinary man's TV and not having Sky. I still don't have it, which is unusual for a football fan but I figured that I'd always be out at a football match when they'd be showing one so I wouldn't get the benefit. That's completely wrong of course, as Murray will no doubt argue, but it suits me. This being the case, Murray knew all about the show and I didn't.

They put us up in a hotel near Heathrow on the Friday night and we had to be at the studio just off Gillette Corner for something silly like 6.30 a.m. on the Saturday morning. We have a phrase that is used a lot by Murray and I when we're in our room just before/after lights out which is, 'This is f****** ridiculous' and it must have started around about this time, because it was. We were just a couple of lads from Sheffield making a noise in support of their team and we're going on the national cultural soccer TV show.

We made it to the show on time which is a miracle, considering my time keeping (more about that later). I have this eternal optimism that makes believe that every game we play we will win and that I will always get to somewhere on time even if I set off late. It doesn't work like that but I still do it today and still believe.

Anyway, we did make it and were placed in the 'green room' which was the waiting room for people who were going on the show. We had prepared a gift for the presenter of the show, Helen Chamberlain, which was a Wednesday shirt with her name on and the number 69. We thought it was funny when we took it out of the bag to give her but the number part of it wasn't particularly shown. We got on very well with Helen who we found, to our approval, was/is definitely a genuine football fan. If you support Torquay you have to be genuine, you can't make that up. Did we fancy her? Speak to any fan of the show and the answer is usually the same, we were no different.

The experience was over all too quickly but we played live on the show several times. They must have liked us because we ended up going on the show something like twenty-nine times in all. We met all kinds of people in the Soccer AM 'green room', including those who wouldn't normally spring to mind, Chris Eubank, for example and Nick Hancock, amongst others. There were plenty of footballers, a young Rio Ferdinand for example and John Hendrie in particular was good fun when he entered the green room seconds after one of the lads had just farted. He didn't forget it either, when we saw him a few months later it was his first topic of conversation. It fell neatly into line with dressing room humour, which is more or less what we have in the band. Nobody gets away with anything, any slight slip is seized upon and whoever made it is battered verbally for as long as possible. This may be why we seem to get on with most footballers and celebrities that we've met.

Helen invited us down to Torquay once and so three of us went down and were shown the sights of Torquay staying in a bed and breakfast used by the Torquay apprentices or scholars as they're called now. That was good fun and we enjoyed nightclubbing in Torquay too, something that wouldn't be as easy for Helen to do now as her fame has reached new heights.

The media attention continued and we appeared on the Big Breakfast Show a couple of times with Ant and Dec, who with we were to later make a record. Sharon Davies, the co-host, was very pleasant as was Luther Vandros or was it Alexandre O'Neil (it's a standing joke that I don't know the difference) who asked us directions to the green room on arriving at the studio. 'It's down there mate and they'll give you a badge so that people know who you are!' was the quip, I don't think he got it which may well have been a good thing. We found ourselves put up in a hotel prior to appearing on the show. Now this hotel was bad, it must have been down on the budget for the show, but it really was crap. The service was bad, the rooms were dirty, the sheets were dirty and the bathrooms worse still. Murray and I, who always room together, found ourselves in a room next to Loz and Denton. We were just settling down to sleep, with an early start the next day, when there was a bang on our door, not any old bang but it was like someone trying to knock it down. Up we jumped out of bed, opened the door, but found nothing, nothing at all. We weren't letting that go so we banged on the door of the two guys in the room next door and ran back inside thinking that would be it. How wrong we were as an almighty bang on the partition wall between the two rooms again made us jump with shock and then seek revenge. The metal tea pot hit the wall to be met with something else from the other side a bit louder, so the metal tray hit the wall, again something louder came back. In between noises you could hear a cackle similar to schoolboys sniggering as the competition to out-do the neighbours continued with a chair next to hit the wall, again to be met with something louder. 'Right! Bed, that'll show 'em'. So it was that the bed was lifted and transported battering ram style across the room and into the wall, much to our amusement. That seemed to be the end of it as there was nothing bigger to hurl their way. Remarkably nothing was broken and there wasn't a mark on the wall, how, I don't know but it was probably due to the fact that the hotel was that bad to start with that nobody could tell the difference.

This set a precedent of some great times and good fun in hotels but as with everything that happens of a humorous nature we have one golden rule, there should never, ever, be any 'irrepairable damage,' full stop. There were many incidents of such humour in the early days of the band and many more to come, all over the world.

The interest in the band was still high but we didn't expect to be called up to play at a Rugby League game or what was to follow. The game was a home game for London Broncos at the Stoop in South West London. Having never been to a London Broncos game before, or any Rugby League game for that matter, we didn't know what to expect. Rugby League had just gone through a rebranding process and Super League had been born, this involved a lot more razzmatazz, with dancers and loud music prior to kick off for the pre-match entertainment.

We joined in happily prior to kick off in an attempt to get the crowd going and the game kick off. The day was a Sunday and the game we were at was already a few games into the season. We weren't aware that the residents in the area hadn't been too impressed with the new Super League approach and the loud music ruining their Sundays. So it was that we were approached by an officer of Richmond Council and served with a noise abatement order! We couldn't believe it but it got funnier because they wanted to do it live on Radio 5 so the reporter came up to us with the council officer and he started his statutory speech serving the order on us. It went something like, 'I hereby serve you with..........' and just as he got to that point the ground started to shake and the buildings and trees too. From over the back of the stand and within, what almost appeared like touching distance, Concord emerged in all its glory with its deafening roar making it hard to hear yourself think never mind hear someone trying to serve a noise abatement order. We collapsed with laughter and the reporter couldn't help but recognise the funny side of things. The poor old council official never did finish serving the notice, not on us anyway.

That was our last appearance at the Stoop even though we were booked to play again courtesy of sponsors, Fosters lager. The first time was enough for Soccer AM to get the footage and show us as defecting to the egg chasing game in typical stitch up Soccer AM style, all good fun. Our second scheduled appearance at the Stoop was cancelled because it fell on the same day as the tragic death of Princess Diana when, rightly so, all sporting events were cancelled.

Chapter Three

The band started in 1993 and we didn't miss a Wednesday game, home or away, for the first three years, that is apart from the grounds from were we were banned. Such was our reputation that other teams didn't want us to turn up at their ground and, together with the Wednesday fans, blow their support out of the water. They were mainly misled of course because what usually happened at away games was that the Wednesday fans got going and so did the home support making for a fantastic atmosphere all round, a win win atmosphere at games if you like.

What I started to do to try and pre-empt any ban was to phone the opposition prior to the game to see if they were going to let us in. This would inevitably mean a conversation with the opposition club's Safety Officer - now they are a strange breed. Unfair to tar them all with the same brush but generally they are the ultimate Jobsworth who, because they have so much responsibility, find it is easier to say no because then there's no problem rather than to say yes and risk whatever problem there may be. There weren't any problems only a few miserable opposition fans complaining that we made more noise than them. In fact, usually there were more compliments from opposition fans and staff alike once we'd visited a ground because we brought with us a carnival atmosphere.

The police certainly supported our admission to grounds because they quickly observed a drop in arrests. There was no foul or abusive chanting, nothing aggressive and nothing racist coming from us meaning that the mood of fans had changed. Basically we were too happy supporting our own team and out-singing the opposition to bother with any of that stuff - beating them in the support stakes was enough.

Needless to say we didn't get past some Jobsworths, usually the smaller clubs like Derby and a particularly amusing ban from Sheffield United. If the safety officers were honest and up front then fair enough and some would be, they'd just say, 'Look, if I let the band in our fans will go mad and we'll get lots of complaints for allowing encouragement for the opposition'. Whilst I didn't agree it's hard to argue against that but often when we got banned we would have to listen to pathetic excuses like it's a safety issue. 'You could attack people with your instruments', was one of them. Have they any idea how much we pay for these instruments! Then we would get, 'In the event of an evacuation people wouldn't be able to exit the stadium because we had instruments'. That's how ridiculous it was. In the case of Derby their stadium manager was so blatantly biased and skirting around the issue that we said, "OK, we'll not come", but we bought 5,000 squeaky horns, the type seen a parties, and gave them away to the Wednesday fans at the turnstiles. What a racket that was but the point was made. A similar thing happened at Nottingham Forest when we were banned but this time we got in for the last few minutes. Only to be immediately thrown back out by the stewards.

That particular incident was funny because the stewards picked on one of our elder members, Brian. Brian had contacted us originally when the band started to say that he would see how it developed and may join later, a year later in fact. Well, Brian was a trumpet teacher and band leader (proper band that is) and wasn't shy at telling people either verbally or through his playing that he could actually play properly unlike the rest of us. Brian was an absolute dream when we needed to play something properly for the TV or radio as he could just rattle any tune off and took great pleasure in doing so. He would never want to step out of line but the stewards picked on him because he was at the end of the line and out he went. All very silly but funny at the same time.

Another strange banning came at Everton. Everton was where it all began and what happened when we went back just proved I was right to have the bugle up my jumper on the first occasion. That was because we were given the all clear by the safety officer to attend Wednesday's fixture there, for which we were grateful. So the match started and we were playing along in the usual way and fortunately went in at half time ahead 2-0.

That was when we were approached by the police and an officer was instructed to stand in-between us to make sure we didn't play at all in the second half under the threat of being arrested. We still won the game but I suppose from an Everton point of view they were seen to do all they could by stopping us, bizarre as it was.

Sunderland was another funny one. Again we were given permission to attend but when we got there we were told of the FA ruling that only allows music to be played when the ball is out of play. Those familiar with this will know that this refers to music played through the speakers in the stadium, so those grounds who have goal music when they score for example will know that when the ball is placed on the penalty spot to take the kick off again the music has to stop. The Sunderland safety officer had deemed we were the same as stadium speakers so were only allowed to play when the ball went out of play. Stewards were dispatched to watch us and make sure that we did just this. Being up for a laugh we decided to make the most of this so we sat down until the ball went out then would stand up and play as much of a tune as we could until the ball came back into play before sitting back down. This could be a matter of seconds if it was a throw in and the crowd would just start to sing the song and stop too. Once the word got round as to why this was happening the fans were only too keen to join in and show the situation up for what it was. The performance had the desired affect and we were told later on in the game, 'Just do what you like, it's OK". Nice chap the Sunderland safety officer too.

The band travelled the country and together with the fans had some great times at Liverpool, Manchester United, Tottenham, Chelsea, Aston Villa, Leeds, Blackburn, West Brom, to name a few. The games at Chelsea and Leeds were notable for different reasons and little did I know at the time would be linked, in a weird way, as I would later end up working for Leeds with Ken Bates as my boss.

The Chelsea game is remembered because we went two goals behind quite early on but we sensed that the fans and the players were up for having a real good go that day. We started to play and rally the troops on and off the field and boy how they joined in. We played non-stop for all the second half, relentlessly drumming and blowing in the hope that we could pull something back from the jaws of defeat. It was one of those games where you knew something was going to happen and it did. We did score in the second half, the second goal coming in injury time to send us all wild. Surprise, surprise we were banned from going again the next year but I was able to discuss it with Ken Bates a number of years later, much to my amusement, as he told of that drum banging away underneath him in the director's box.

The Leeds incident was funny for a different reason. We'd gone to Elland Road, one of Wednesday's biggest rivals, after Sheffield United of course, and blown them away with the noise that was generated by the Wednesday fans that day. Again we won and had to return to our car for the short trip home down the M1. Getting back to the car is always a tricky moment at an away ground but with instruments you can hardly hide, easier with a trumpet but a drum or euphonium there's no chance of getting them up your jumper. We walked from the away end down Elland Road towards the car park to be met by loads of abusive Leeds fans coming in the opposite direction which only added to the satisfaction of winning that day really. The icing on the cake came though when one Leeds fan stopped and said, 'Ah, that's the drum is it?' Always a silly question if you ask me given that it clearly is and its been heard for the last 90 minutes but it is surprising how many times we get it. Not content with asking silly questions he started to kick the drum, obviously hurting his foot but he also began to blame the drum and kick it as if it had been playing itself and it was most amusing to all watching, including Leeds fans. What a prize pudding he was! The drum survived and Murray, the drummer, whose fault it actually was came under no threat whatsoever.

The band had grown in size now and we had our first female member, Julie, who played trombone. Julie was a season ticket holder and would travel down from Driffield on home match days which confirmed what we were looking for which is proper fan first and musical ability second. Julie though was a good player too and contributed a great deal. There would be many a time when although quiet we would catch her laughing to herself at the banter and antics that we all got up to. There were now about eight or nine of us with Me, Murray, Loz, Denton, Julie, Brian, Jimmy (a drummer) and Max another drummer. Then Bram joined us. Bram is a smashing chap who had retired from the bank some years earlier and had bought himself a saxophone. He responded to an advert in the programme and met up with us. As with all auditions for the band the test was are you a proper fan first before you can play and Bram had been a season ticket holder for more years than we'd been alive, so he was in. As it happens he can play as well as any of us, so that worked too.

Bram, who we know is 83 years old, related to us how when he gets home he tells the rest of his family about the antics he's been getting up to and what we'd been doing, much to the disbelief of his wife and offspring because, I suppose, they'd always known him as the bank manager, who was a bank manager when bank managers were just what it said on the tin. He gained extra respect when he told us that he'd served in the Navy in the second world war and when we discovered that he could recite all the words to 'there'll always be and England'. Absolute salt of the earth is Bram, top, top man and later he was nicknamed Emperor Bram, a title that is well deserved and very fitting.

Bram would have approved of our first national newspaper coverage that was a near full page feature in The Times. It was a very fair article and quite satisfying to be featured in a 'proper' newspaper. However, there was a part of the article that referred to how refreshing it was that here were a group of football fans travelling around the country supporting their team with no commercialisation involved at all at a time when all around football was changing with the advent of the Premier League and all. That inference was very true at the time but was later to change through necessity, I hope the journalist doesn't feel betrayed in any way.

In the very early days when the local sports paper, the Green Un, were featuring us regularly I was asked to appear on a record by Loz, Denton and Denton's mate, Ian, who were in a band and practiced just off Bramall Lane of all places. At the same time they asked if I could contact Tango man, Sheffield Wednesday's crazy super fan, to appear as well. I duly did this and we made the record with the main features being the bugle and Tango talking over a piano track played by Loz.

Loz and I go back a long way, in fact about 42 years or so, including playing in the same football team (the one that won the Sanderson Trophy when we were 10 years old) and we had many good times at school together, getting up to mischief. Loz is one of the funniest people you could ever meet. Unfortunately he got caught up in something that none of us wanted to be caught up in which was from my interpretation just not right.

In short when the record was made it was put on to cassettes (remember those) and we thought it had the potential to sell a few copies. To produce 2,000 copies we needed funding and a means of selling the cassettes. I funded the production to the tune of £2,000 and went around local shops to see if they would stock them to sell. This also involved putting 2,000 inserts into cassette cases one night at Loz's house. Murray was there but others were missing when the work was needed to be done. Needless to say I never got my money back although we sold quite a few copies, probably about half of what we had. So, when a minor record label, Cherry Red Records, came knocking on the door to see if we would allow the record to be included in their football anthems album, I didn't think there would be a problem. I was wrong and it was a lesson learned about 'rock and roll'. There was no payment involved unless the record sold millions which was never going to happen but people became very precious about their involvement and quite a rumpus occurred about what appeared on the wording of the album. Looking back the whole thing was a joke and should have been fun. The record was quite good and Tango's bit too but he never got a look in! It ended up a mess which was a shame.

Tango would often appear at the same photo shoots as us when the press were involved around Sheffield Wednesday and he is a great lad with a wicked sense of humour. His motivation is the same as ours just to spur on the team by his antics and it works. The funniest time we were together was when some magazine, Match of the Day I think, wanted to shoot him painted orange, so we turned up on the pitch at Hillsborough to witness Tango, stripped half naked as usual, in the back of the net posing for the photographer (snapper to the initiated) with his entire body painted orange. This in itself wasn't entirely unexpected, what was unexpected was that when we'd finished the orange paint wouldn't come off no matter how much rubbing took place. Tango (Paul) went into the changing rooms to try and get the paint off and emerged just the same with a cheeky grin on his face indicating that he was quite enjoying it really. What the snapper didn't realise was that Tango is from Wolverhampton and had to drive all the way home from Sheffield as an orange man. The next time we saw him he had plenty of stories of double takes from people driving past him, including from the police, and, being a coach driver he had more stories when he turned up to work still painted. Apparently it took more than a week to come off in the end.

Our next foray into the record making business was with Martyn Ware and Ian Reddington, both big Wednesday supporters who had made a record together a few years earlier to celebrate Big Ron's Wednesday teams appearing at Wembley in the early 90's. Martyn is a member of Heaven 17 and Ian, now as then, a successful actor playing both Tricky Dicky in East Enders and Vernon in Coronation Street and it was at a Wednesday away game that I saw them and approached them to say, 'Isn't it time we made a record together?' to which they replied, 'Yes, it is'.

So after a few trips to London and the cementing of a good friendship our first CD was produced, named, 'Oh Yes!' The CD was sold in the SWFC club shop and again didn't make any money but we were just happy to have a good CD for sale and in the club shop too. It stayed on sale for a very long time in the shop, probably because they had too many to sell. We took some satisfaction, small as it was, that the club did make a bit of profit on selling the CD, so we'd made some kind of financial contribution to the club we love.

More records were to come but we'd learned very early on in our record making career that you're not going to get rich making records, especially if you finance it yourself and have no distribution chain but that wasn't what it was all about. It was genuinely all about a

41

bit of fun. We promised ourselves at this time and many times since that we started the band as a means of support for the team and to be a laugh and that this was how it was going to stay, records or no records.

So we had started to unwittingly create a group of fans, all of the same mind and would meet up at away games not by arrangement but because that's what we did. We travelled the length and breadth of the country as football fans do and usually out-shouted the opposition wherever we were but there was one occasion that stands out above all others and that was away at Norwich City. We had really pushed the boat out with getting the word around that we (and the 'we' were the fans not just the band) were having a Honalulu Beach Party at Norwich that would involve fans wearing grass skirts, Hawaiian shirts garlands and carrying anything that was inflatable. 2,000 skirts were acquired and sold like hot cakes along with blue and white garlands and inflatables included air beds, alligators, hammers, beach balls, arm bands you name it. The away end was sold out with some 2,200 plus Wednesday fans making the not too easy trip to Norwich.

There must have been something in the air that warm end of season day because the fans were in the ground early and all started singing before 2.30 p.m. We don't normally start playing until kick off because we like the element of surprise for the opposition and also because what we do is extremely knackering after 90 minutes, never mind an extra half hour! It didn't seem to matter that day and the crowd kept singing with inflatables flying through the air at every end and turn. One poor steward had the misfortune to walk in front of the stand only half looking at the crowd. Some fan had spotted this and crept up on him with the inflatable alligator thrusting it at him at the last minute and near frightening him to death, much to the amusement of the crowd. The teams came out for the warm up and the crowd sang on, they kicked off and the crowd sang on. In fact, the crowd sang on throughout the whole of the first half at full volume as the band played continuously. The game seemed secondary, even though, of course, we wanted to win, such was the performance by the fans. Half time usually signals time to have a rest, go to the toilet get a drink, not on this occasion. Nobody stopped, no one, right through half time. The teams went off, had their break and came back on to the same continuous full on noise, there could not have been any more noise coming from any set of fans anywhere ever. The second half kicked off and the Honolulu party continued and by now the Norwich fans were transfixed by the activity coming from the away end. Norwich even scored and it made no difference whatsoever to the support that day, I'm sure that some fans don't even know a goal had been scored, even now. This incredible sound continued throughout the second half and then the final whistle sounded and we'd lost 1-0, no matter, the Wednesday fans sang and we played on until after 5.30 p.m. a full 45 minutes after the game had finished and we only stopped then because the stewards made us leave. It was an awesome day and you may think it had finished then, but no, much to our amazement the Norwich fans were so fascinated by what had happened that they had lined the street outside the ground and as we started to play again with the fans in full voice they applauded us up the street and around the ground back to our cars, now that never happens anywhere. How do I know it was awesome, because anyone who was there still remembers it to this day. Norwich fans flooded the club with letters and even our own directors, who were on the other side of the ground that day, stayed behind to witness it and took the trouble to make a big thing of it, something else that does not usually happen. That was a day that will go down in history for us.

There were though, to be many things that would happen in the not-too-distant future and what we'd been used to so far, on a local scale, was nothing compared to the roller coaster we were about to board........

Chapter Four

England was buzzing with excitement about international football in 1996 following Euro '96 and the fact that England should really have qualified and won the tournament. It was a time of Skinner and Baddeal, 'Football's coming home' and Gazza at his best. The disappointment that England fans have often felt was evident in the country then as it was in previous years and has been since, when our national team play in major tournaments; however, we England fans maintain the belief that we will win every tournament that we enter and that's how it is. No logic, no reasoning, we just believe it because......OK?

Terry Venables had left his role as national team manager and Glenn Hoddle was appointed as the new boss at the beginning of the 1996/97 season. Murray and I found ourselves at Highbury watching Wednesday play Arsenal, a game that usually meant defeat and built on the history of games between the clubs which included the marathon men cup run of 1978 and two cup finals in

1993, all lost games. In fact we always seemed to lose to Arsenal, if it wasn't at Hillsborough, that was. That midweek night we were at Highbury, full of optimism and ready to give our all, Murray as usual on the drum and me on the trumpet but knowing at the back of our minds that we hadn't won away at Arsenal for about 30 years (now closer to 45!)

We were a good side then although a little on the slide from the cup final sides of a few years earlier. Arsenal always seem to have been a good side and this was a team headed by Ian Wright who was their top scorer and many other internationals. The game kicked off and so did we as the band. Much to our pleasure we scored early on in the game so this was it, this was the game that I'd been waiting for all my life. Not just me but Murray and all the other fans there that night we were about to beat Arsenal. When something like this happens you go mad as football fans and I blew the trumpet and Murray banged the drum with every last bit of energy we had. We were knackered after a very short while but as was the case on many previous occasions the adrenalin kicked in and enabled us to just go for it. '1-0 to the Arsenal was the song of the time because they always seemed to win 1-0.1-0 to the Arsenal my arse! To quote a Jim Royle phrase, we were winning and loving it. The fans and the band were in fine form with the rest of the ground watching the antics and being out shouted as we finally found ourselves in front, away at Arsenal.

As time progressed the game changed and history started to repeat itself Arsenal equalised. Not only did they equalise they scored another, 2-1 to them, then another, 3-1 and finally the fourth making it 4-1 to them. It was one of those times when OK, we've lost 4-1 but we've given more as fans than the opposition fans did and it wasn't as bad as when I'd travelled back from a work trip to Holland, re routed to Heathrow for the return flight, crossed London and begged a lift back to Sheffield with friends only to end up losing again and 7-0 that time!

We left Highbury that night bitterly disappointed again and hoping, as is still the case today, that one day we'll beat Arsenal away, one day, one day I hope, in my life time, please.

The next day was work as usual selling and hiring out commercial vehicles in the Yorkshire area. I was driving along the M62 when my very large mobile phone rang and it was David Davis the Chief Executive of the Football Association, not a call one would expect. He said that he had been at Highbury the previous evening with Glenn Hoddle who was watching the players with a view to picking his first England squad. They were so impressed with what we were doing with the band, the reaction we were getting from the crowd and the difference we were making to the atmosphere that he asked, 'Would you like to play for England?

It was a time when you could drive and speak on the phone legally and I don't mind admitting that when I got the call I filled up, I was so overwhelmed that I had to pull over on to the hard shoulder, tears trickling down my cheeks. From being a kid imagining playing for England at Wembley and then not realising the dream as a footballer, but, to be then asked that question as a fan was the next best thing. To be asked to play for England was an honour and for it to come from the Chief Executive of the FA at his and the England manager's request, it was just the best endorsement and honour that we could ever have wished for.

Once I'd pulled myself together I couldn't say yes quickly enough. The FA would sort us out with tickets and a mini bus for the first game v Poland which was fantastic. It was brilliant that our efforts in supporting our team had been recognised at a national level, this had been done by following the team home and away and as far as we were concerned this was the way that we would support England. We are proper football fans, home and away is the way you support and that was it. We also decided from the beginning that we would endeavour to be as little hassle to the FA as possible and that we didn't want any special treatment regarding away tickets. To this end and to this day we pay for our tickets and travel, obtaining tickets via what is now the 'englandfans' club like every other fan. Fans don't like 'free loaders', if we're all in it together, all the same, there's a mutual respect that exists between real fans. That's how we wanted it and it is how it is. A later slogan of the FA was Alltogether Now, absolutely right.

It was like the starter's pistol had gone off. I told Murray and the other lads, who were just ecstatic, 'Over the Moon', a well used football phrase fitting the bill very nicely. The reason for the starter's gun analogy was that the press got hold of the story immediately with The Sun first off the mark. Before we knew it they'd sent a photographer to take a picture of us at my house and a now familiar process began. That being, if you're in the paper one day the radio pick it up the next and the TV after that.

I woke up the day after the Sun photo had been taken and went to the newsagents to buy the paper to see what they'd put on us. I bought a paper and started to scan through the paper from the front, (unusual because as a football fan you always start at the back). I went through the entire paper and found nothing, nothing that was until I adopted the football fan approach and turn to the back page. The entire back page was about us, the photo from the house the night before with the headline 'Glenn's Band of Hope and Glory' covered the whole page, unbelievable!

It seemed then that every form of media wanted their share of the story. So we found ourselves on the local radio stations again, Sky TV, BBC and ITV in all the papers and on Radio 5, Radio 4 and Virgin Radio.

The Radio 4 piece was particularly interesting because their listeners aren't normally football friendly and the piece involved their reporter coming up to Wakefield where I worked and recording the interview with me playing various tunes on the trumpet. All trumpeters know that it is very difficult to play 'from cold' so one needs to warm up which I did. The reporter chose to record the warm up as well as the tunes and did the interview with me. I learned another lesson where some of the media are concerned and in particular this reporter because when the programme was aired the warm up

49

session was portrayed as our tunes thus ridiculing what is our limited talent. Very naughty, Radio 4, but you live and learn. Mainly not to be too precious and to accept that there are naughty people in the media who will stitch you up but in our case we are lucky because going back to another one of our catch phrases, 'The guy on the terrace is not Pavarotti and we are not the Halle orchestra'. Very fortunate in our case because they can stitch us up all they want, it's not like we're going to lose out on record sales or concert ticket sales.

All in all we couldn't have been happier with the prospect of playing for our country and the day fast approached. We hired the mini bus which turned out to be a limousine for the same price. Wouldn't be seen dead in a limousine today but it was a bit of a novelty then so we went for it. The other thing was that we didn't know how our debut was going to go or if we would be accepted, if it would go well and therefore if we would be asked back. We wanted to make the most fantastic atmosphere ever and certainly make it such that the opposition wondered what had hit them, if not on the first game as quickly as possible. The FA had sent us some clothing to wear for which we were grateful, some off it good stuff from Umbro and some a bit outsized but this was England clothing so it didn't matter.

Six of us made the journey down to Wembley that day, Wednesday, 9th October 1996 for the World Cup qualifying game at home to Poland. Two drums and four brass players turned up at Wembley, as instructed, a minimum of three hours before kick off. The limo was parked in the Wembley car park and we met a guy from the FA, John Egglestaff, who was our contact and Mark Armstrong who took us to our seats and a wonderful lady called Barbara, with a great sense of humour, who was on reception. Barbara gave us a packed lunch each, and again we were very grateful. The FA really couldn't have looked after us any better and we were made very welcome. So we'd made it to the stadium, Wembley stadium, twin towers and all. I'd been before for England matches most memorably v Scotland, Holland and Argentina but it was the first time for some of the lads. It was also a time when England games attracted a fair number of hooligans. As proper football fans of several years and not exactly shrinking violets ourselves we were ready for any eventuality that night and so it was that we would found ourselves in front of a group of, said hooligans, from Millwall when the game kicked off.

The band started to play and there wasn't much response at all. This was a new thing to everyone at the time and they just weren't used to it. The abuse came from the group of 'idiots' who had found out that we were from the north which added to the rivalry. To make matters worse Poland scored quite early on in the game to give them a 1-0 lead. At that time I can remember thinking that's all we need, not just because it was our debut but because we wanted a win full stop. We knew it would be a harder task to generate a good atmosphere when we were one nil down but we stuck at it.

We stuck at it and the crowd joined in particularly with the drums. The 'idiots' behind us saw us as a target for banter as we would probably have done if it were the other way round but they got as good as they were giving, more so from those of us who were a bit more savvy regarding crowd banter. Basically they were trying to find out what we were like? If we were willing to be victimised then they would do it. So, we gave all the answers that say, actually we're alright, we're proper fans, we know the crack so shut up and pick on someone else or be ready to get shown up because we're very good at terrace banter, very good indeed. Denton, the plonker, even lost his drum stick to one of them but we played on regardless and then Shearer banged one in 1-1, the game had turned. Thank God for that, the crowd around us were ecstatic, as were we, even the idiots were happy. The crowd joined in more and more as the game continued and gradually we won them over. Whether this had any influence on the pitch no one knows but it wasn't long before we scored again. The crowd sang until the final whistle and we had won. Our first game as the England Band and we'd won at Wembley what an awesome feeling.

Outside the stadium after the game a carnival atmosphere ensued as we decided to play in celebration of the victory. In truth it was probably too much of a carnival atmosphere as it blocked the top of Wembley Way causing a bit too much congestion. TV crews were out in force filming the after match celebrations that were broadcast nationwide. Eventually we made it back through the crowds to the car and our first match was complete. The long journey up the M1 wasn't complete but that didn't seem to matter so much after that first win. The feeling of elation, and of satisfaction that we had hopefully contributed to the win, in some small way, and of course that we had won, was second to none.

Back to work the next day but it didn't feel the same, a bit if a come-down really but the phone did keep ringing with press enquiries. If the truth be known the phone rang too much with press enquiries and not enough with work enquiries. The business I had was my own car and van rental business so there was no one there to tell me to stop concentrating on the band and start concentrating on work. The business ticked over and gave me the freedom to do what needed doing with the band or more truthfully what I wanted to do, which was anything to do with the band. We did some crazy things looking back. One such example was that we were contacted by Channel 4 to see if we would go on a programme called 'Under the Moon'. Great, of course we would. There was no payment for going on, I'm not even sure there were expenses, the show started at midnight, hence the 'Under the moon' title. It started at midnight but didn't finish until 2am and it was in London at the Channel 4 studios. By the time we were clear of the studio it was often 2.30 a.m. or 3.00 a.m. and we faced a three hour drive back to Sheffield. 6.00 a.m. to bed and up at 7.00 a.m. The thing is we didn't just do this once or twice we did it several times and we enjoyed it too.

One time, Murray, myself and Jimmy (another drummer - student, don't go there) went down and found the studio in the usual way, just past the Houses of Parliament, roundabout, turn right and it's there on the right. We were waiting to go on the show looking out of the window into the street at about 1.00 a.m. when an old Saab car came screeching round the corner mounted the kerb and parked right in front of the studio. 'Look at that. Who the hell's that?' someone cried, as this figure bounded out of the car and up to the front door with an obvious confidence and clearly not giving much of a toss for parking regulations.

A few minutes later as we were sat in the Green Room waiting to go on the show the door flung open and this smiling almost laughing figure stood there and said, 'OK who's got the fags then?' To our amazement it was Jo Brand! Jimmy quick as a flash and being the only smoker jumped to his feet and disappeared with Jo down the corridor to wherever they smoke. When they came back to the Green Room we had quite a laugh and must say that Jo Brand was just the same as you would imagine, same as on TV.

The show was hosted by Danny Kelly who was extremely nervous presenting the show but what a clever feller, ask him any stat on football and it's there. We'd first met Danny when we were asked to go on to Radio 5's 606 show when it was hosted by another top man, Danny Baker. Why is Danny Baker a top man? Because he's one of us, a proper football fan and a genuine bloke. When we first met we'd speak of memories of previous matches between Millwall and Sheffield Wednesday and of what turned out to be shared experiences and characters that we knew. Harry the Dog being one famous Millwall 'hooligan' that we both came across in our youth, Danny more than me of course but luckily for him he was on the same side.

When we went on the 606 show it was chaos and radio genius, Danny Baker, loved it. A full band in a very small studio of about ten feet square and playing at will, as loud as possible, often relating to the caller that was on air, so a Portsmouth fan would get a Pompey song, etc., etc. Great fun as was the case the next time.

The next time came about because Danny said, 'Whenever you are in London pop in', so we did. Sheffield Wednesday were away at West Ham so we turned up at the Talk Sport studios on Oxford Street after the game. Why Talk Sport? Because he'd moved stations. 'We're here for the Danny Baker Show,' we said to the security guard on duty at the entrance.

'I don't have you down.'

'Oh don't worry about that kid, give him a call.'

He rang the studio who let us in but didn't tell him. What a laugh it was bursting in on him in the studio live on air. After the show he took us down the road to the pub and we chatted more about football, proper football. Great reception, great fun, great bloke and our paths would cross again a few years later when we made a couple of appearances on the TFI Friday TV show that he was involved in with Chris Evans.

England's next game was a World Cup qualifying game away in Georgia and try as we might we couldn't get tickets for the game. It was a month after our Wembley debut and had simply arrived too soon for us to join the England fans club which would have enabled us to get tickets and book the transport but that was the last time we were to be caught out, we weren't going to let it happen again. Not for a competitive game anyway. England won 2-0 which set up the next game very well, that being at home to Italy our main rivals in the qualifying group.

Italian football was more fashionable in the late 90s with Serie A supposedly the place to play, with the best atmosphere in the grounds. We just saw this as a challenge especially as when we formed originally in 1993 Trevor Francis had sited Italian fans as ones who could create a great atmosphere from his time with Sampdoria as a player. We were well up for the challenge when the game arrived and we'd made the trip south with great anticipation knowing that if we won this game we were well on the way to qualifying for the World Cup Finals in France 1998. The game was a sell-out as all England games now seemed to be after Euro '96. We struck up the band and the crowd joined in immediately. The atmosphere was electric but Italy were a good side, better than their fans effort that night. The English crowd out-shouted the Italians that night and the team fought hard but the Italians played like their league sides do and scraped a 1-0 victory having defended all evening. The result was that Italy and England were then neck and neck with each other at the top of the World Cup qualifying group.

A friendly match against Mexico a month later further familiarised fans with our tunes and they got to know us a bit more as we did them. The thing being that at club level we saw the same fans every week sometimes twice a week, so getting to know new songs and chants was easy after a couple of games. It could be done in two or three weeks. This was the case with what we call the 'Italian' which was later knicked as far as we're concerned by Dario Gee and Fat Les and turned into hit records. Apparently Dario Gee even credited us for making it popular but he got the number 2 hit and all the money as did Fat Les (Keith Allen) who we were later to meet up with and have the discussion. Tango actually deserves the credit for introducing the song into popular terrace culture because he went on a Sheffield Wednesday pre season tour to Holland and came back raving about this tune. He sang it to us at a Wednesday away match at Coventry and that was it probably one of the most popular terrace tunes ever was born. It was clear that with England fans it was going to take a little longer to familiarise everyone with what we did and not only that the home crowd changed so much from game to game. There is a hard core of England fans of course but particularly at home games there are a lot of very welcome fans who maybe visit just once a year or even once a lifetime. We had to think of a way of getting round this problem so the thinking caps were on.

Next up were Georgia in another very important World Cup qualifying game again at Wembley and again a lot of press interest prior to the game. We needed to win to keep level with Italy at the top of the group and interest in England was again very high. It was at this time that, The Sun, who had earlier dubbed us, 'Glenn's Band of Hope and Glory,' started to take a greater interest in us and assigned a reporter, Antonella Lazzerri, to look after us and make us an offer that we couldn't refuse. Basically, the offer was that for a few photos and quotes they'd organise and pay for our travel to away games. Like any other group of lads and lass (not forgetting Julie, our trombonist) we were as skint as the next and some of the band members simply couldn't afford to travel away to every England game so we gladly accepted. We had a few photos taken outside Wembley and played a few tunes outside to get the crowd in the mood. We should have known better really with the resulting crowd congestion rightly getting us into trouble again and we were asked not to play close to the stadium before games in future. There were always a lot of school trips to England games and the kids loved it when the band struck up. This was a time before every kid had a mobile phone so often it was a big group asking for a photo, requests that we would duly fulfil. We received many letters from different schools thanking us for our efforts that contributed towards them having had a great time. One school from Bristol said that their kids, who were sat near us, sang throughout the whole match, then back to the coach and then sang all the way home (and the M4 is a very long road), they thoroughly enjoyed it. We were and still are flattered by positive comments we get although these are seen as a by product of what we do which is just trying to create the best possible atmosphere we can at games.

England brushed aside Georgia with a 2-0 victory and we went home, in the limo, very happy. The limo trips had become events in themselves with ten of us squashed in together. Three seats at the front and back of the car and a long four seater in between down one side. A few friendly rivalries were building up in the band which would spill over on these long trips home. Some, probably Loz (still one of the funniest blokes you will ever meet, if you know him), found that there was a switch that turned all the lights out in the back of the car and it was pitch black when this happened. As soon as this was discovered, out it went, and apples, water, ping pong balls (yes) and anything else that we could get our hands on flew down form end to end whacking whoever, but mainly aimed at Denton, in the head. This would be followed by raids on various positions in the car and a few slaps, pile ups and wrestling matches all in the dark. It was at its height completely mad and hysterical and quite knackering but very funny despite the minor injuries.

Our regular appearances on Soccer AM continued and this was the time when we had Helen Chamberlain, Sky Soccer AM presenter, playing with us on drums. Helen had played the drum for Torquay previously so absolutely understood what we were all about and was a welcome addition. Helen even managed to persuade us to go to two Torquay away games at Hull and Mansfield, in the then fourth division, to play in support of Torquay. They were both mid week games and praise indeed for those Torquay fans that made it to the games, certainly at the Mansfield game there were more of us in the band than there were Torquay supporters. Fortunately for Helen but unfortunately as far as the band were concerned when it came to Wembley games, Helen's increasing popularity meant that it was becoming impossible for her to sit in the stand with us and play. Over enthusiastic autograph hunters and admirers would crowd around continually during the game so Helen's short band career reluctantly came to an end after three or four games.

Another welcome guest who accompanied us to a game at the old Wembley was Alan Plater, the renowned playwright, who had written many things, form Z cars to Selwyn Frogitt and A Very British Coup, to name but a few. Far more renowned that I realised when I contacted him to see if he would be interested in writing a play/film or anything about the lads from Sheffield who ended up playing at Wembley. He did and again he was someone who understood what we were about instantly. Alan liked what he saw and wrote a sitcom that he sent to Yorkshire TV. The first episode featured me as a plumber and Murray as an unemployed man answering an advert to join the band by coming round to my house at midnight banging the drum and scaring my wife (who I didn't have at the time really) to death. The upshot being we both got arrested for disturbing the peace in the first show. The sitcom hasn't been made yet and Alan pointed out to me at the time, when I rang him on a weekly/daily basis, that he'd just had a play that was to star Judy Dench take twelve years to come to the screen, which means I should give him another call about now!

Most of the lads in the band had girlfriends at the time and inevitably there was a strain on our relationships with the amount of time we spent on band activities, especially when it used to cost us quite a bit too. The brass instruments are expensive and the way we played and treated them meant that they needed renewing quite frequently as we didn't spend very much on them initially. After literally blowing up several trumpets due to the volume that we play at, I bit the bullet and laid out £1500 to get a very substantially made, thicker grade, silver trumpet that has now lasted at least six years. The bigger cost was to relationships. We were always away either at a Wednesday match or England game or on TV/ radio and if we were at home certainly I'd be on the phone organising the next match or trip. In the early days of the band I was player/manager of the local Sunday football team, Stannington Village, with some success winning the League Cup, in addition to the band which, looking back, all added up to a recipe for disaster relationship wise. This was echoed in Murrays situation too because whatever we did we always did together as a band and must have been the case with all the other lads to varying degrees. The nightmare situation was when two or more girlfriends got together away from us because we both knew we were in for an ear bashing when we got in, fully justified but we loved what we were doing and still do, so the sympathy and concern that maybe should have been there, wasn't. This situation, of our own creation, willingly riding the wave of any media attention and ending up more skint than ever, neglecting work, my closing the rental office early and being away from base a lot, doing something for nothing, instead of earning and Murray blagging off work when he should have been working probably had a hand in both Murray and myself starting to stray a little on the relationship front.

I remember going to watch 'Fever Pitch' at the cinema and half way through thinking, this film could be about me, a guy totally obsessed with football to the point of neglecting his partner. When I turned to look at my former girlfriend she had realised the same thing as the flood of tears running down her cheeks testified. I suppose the writing was on the wall.

Old Trafford was the venue for England v South Africa, this game was a precursor for when Wembley was to close for redevelopment and all England games would be 'on the road' meaning they would be hosted at various grounds around the country. The atmosphere was better than normal for a friendly, whether this was seen as the chance for northern fans to show what they could do compared to a southern crowd I don't know but they certainly responded that day and a fine 2-1 victory resulted.

After this game we were into another vitally important game if England were to qualify for the World Cup in France a year later in 1998. Whether it was our connection with The Sun, or just coincidence, I don't know but we found ourselves invited to appear on Virgin Radio on the Monday of the week that England were playing Poland away in Krakov. The Russ and Jonno show was very popular in London and nationally on medium wave only but still popular. Three of us went to London for the show myself, Murray and Jimmy i.e. one trumpet and two drums. When we got to No.1 Golden Square we found that we were on the show with none other than, The Stranglers, who I'd been a fan of in my youth, Golden Brown and all that, OK, they're not The Clash but it was still interesting to meet them. Disappointingly they were nice, gone were the days of gobbing on everyone a few years earlier. We got on well with the staff at Virgin, so much so that they asked if we were going to Poland on Saturday or more to the point would we like to go to Poland with them for the England game? They had been offered a trip by a Polish Brewery company called EB who were paying for the lot. These things happen, but not to us, however, this one did and we were on that plane at Luton airport a few days later to Krakov. The instruments were out on the plane for a few tunes, we even had a visit to the cockpit at the pilot's request. The Virgin lot were a fantastic group of lads and lasses and we quickly learned that they were in the middle of a potential buy-out by Capital Radio. Their apparently realistic fear was that this could be their last trip together because if Capital were successful they could all lose their jobs, worrying times but this was their blow out and all paid for by a brewery with as much beer as anyone would want to drink. I kept it quiet that I am teetotal, yes, I am teetotal.

The first part of the trip was a reception in the Town Hall with a banquet of Polish food laid on for us. We were all grateful but there's only so much pickled stuff you can eat so we ended up in a very dodgy underground nightclub. A group of shaven headed bruisers were following us around dressed in black overcoats, about six of them, everybody moved when they approached us and the Poles. We needn't have worried, they were our group's minders, assigned to look after us if needed. By the way people reacted they were very well known and obviously instilled fear. We had two days to go before the game so the next day we were to go on a tour of the castle in the town but we were woken up by Russ Williams banging on the door. We'd over-slept and were late for the breakfast trip to McDonalds so we scrambled around frantically, got dressed and met them in the McDonalds. This was Poland just after they had broken away from the rest of the iron curtain countries and everybody appeared to be as miserable as could be. All the cars were Trabants or Moscavichs but McDonalds had arrived and it was packed, no wonder, the prices were unbelievably cheap, I suppose they have to be when nobody has any money.

The castle tour in Krakov centre was interesting, as interesting as it could be after the night we'd had, then we headed back to the hotel where the Virgin Radio crew were in full swing in one of the rooms. How many people can you get in one room? They were all bollocksed on EB beer, well almost all of them and very funny as they started, for some reason, to worship a chair in the room holding it high above their heads. As they do in these situations things began to get out of hand a little as the clothes of one of the lads in the room were thrown out of the window, then some other things, the chair was about to go with rumours about the television. Time to leave, so we did hastily.

The next day was match day so the instruments were out in the hotel foyer and we played on the coach on the way to the game to a full chorus. It was freezing so we kept moving on the way to the stadium intrigued by the fact that the Polish fans all wore Harrington jackets, had a skin head and a Rottweiler dog. How they were going to get in the match with those we didn't know. Our group, plus the bouncers who were looking after us, entered the stadium and we ran up the steps to the open roofed terrace. To our amazement and it has to be said concern we were in the Polish end. The England fans were to our left in the segregated area as is normal to prevent crowd trouble but we were right in the middle of the Polish hooligans! There were enough of us to get noticed by the Polish and by the England fans across the pitch. Oh well, 'In for a penny in for a pound'. We started playing, the national anthem was a cracker with our group in full voice and the England fans acknowledging us from afar. Then it was kick-off in front of us, but it was the Poles fighting each other. Another quick learning curve for us was that at Poland's international games there was a problem at the time between rival fans fighting each other from domestic clubs. What a relief that was for us, our Polish guards had told us that although it looked bad they were more bothered about them beating each other up with scaffolding poles than they were about us. So what a situation we were in, we could play all we wanted and get our group singing and encourage the team from two sides of the ground as England fans. England were brilliant that night delivering a well played for 2-0 victory and another step closer to qualifying for France '98. We were ecstatic.

What we learned later from the England fans in the segregated section was that we'd gained a bit of a hero status in the bravery stakes as far as they were concerned. They could see all this fighting going on around us with flares, police and groups running up and down the terrace and yet they could still hear the National Anthem and Rule Britannia bombing out. The real situation was different of course but we were happy to take the new found credibility and go with them. Afterwards I'd never seen such a number of police-vans escorting the England fans down the road, as we rode past on the coach. It must have been at least a mile long, nose to tail, with the night sky lit up in blue because of the hundreds of flashing blue lights. What mattered to us was the victory and we'd, hopefully, done a decent job again on the terraces. Come on England!

The next couple of England games were both friendlies with France and Brazil, a kind of mini tournament to keep the players fit that took place in France. We beat France 1-0 and lost to Brazil 0-1. However, the games that we were looking forward to were the next World Cup qualifying games v Moldova at Wembley and the showdown with Italy in Rome.

Chapter Five

In the end Virgin Radio was bought by Chris Evans and not by Capital so our new found friends needn't have worried at all about their jobs as they ended up all being safe. We did keep in touch with Russ Williams and even met up with him when Wednesday played Tottenham at White Hart Lane, Russ being a Spurs fan. Again, we'd sussed out the real football fans who we identified with naturally. On another occasion they asked us to surprise a friend of theirs whose birthday it was. They had booked a birthday meal at 'Gabriel's' Restaurant. Gabriel's was in Golden Square, the same as the Virgin Radio studio, so we knew exactly where to turn up. We staked out the joint and waited for everyone to sit down to dinner before busting in. Now let me tell you when we burst into a room of any size, playing at full volume, it is like a bomb has gone off, and as this fact is always at the back of Londoners minds it may have explained the reaction of the diners who jumped out of their skins, some physically leaving their seats and landing again. All good fun when they realised why we were there. However, when we enquired who the birthday girl was there wasn't one. This was a business meeting, the birthday party was downstairs in the basement! Whoops, we'd got the wrong group. Laughing all the way down stairs we did the same thing all over again but this time for the right people.

The next few England games were friendlies with France, Italy and Brazil, in a kind of mini tournament to keep the players fit and familiar with each other through the summer of 1997. The tournament took place in various locations in France.

Our first game was against Italy who beat us 2-0, a very significant result psychologically with both sides knowing that they were to face each other later in the year for what was expected to be a play off to see who qualified automatically for France '98. England also beat France 1-0, however, the World Champions, Brazil, managed to get one over on us winning 1-0 in Paris. These tournaments don't have the same level of competitiveness as a 'proper' tournament. However beating Italy made the tournament worthwhile.

The Italy game in the 'proper' competition was the one that all England fans were looking forward to and we were no exception. However, there was the not so small matter of the more immediate World Cup qualifying game v Moldova at Wembley to contend with first. By now we had another addition to the band that being 'Adolf' (Simon). Adolf was a trumpeter and a welcome addition. Adolf was one of our footballing friends from the village football team and could have made the grade as a pro footballer but his career was cut short through injury when playing for Hartlepool United. Why Adolf?

You may well ask. Well, he was nicknamed Adolf because he was a stickler for everything, but mainly timing. Most unfortunate really because I am one of the world's worst when it comes to time keeping so we would often be late when picking him up which would inevitably lead to the timing conversation. I have to confess I'd do it on purpose sometimes just to see if he could chill out...he couldn't. But finally we had someone who could blow as loud as I could, volume of course being the main requisite of any band member but Adolf could play too, which was a bonus.

The limo was hired again for Wembley and Adolf showed his skill in another more unpleasant area of wind dispersion, seemingly all the way down and back he would fart every five minutes filling the car with his foul smell. A liking of diet coke was to blame, or that was the excuse and he had the cheek to complain about my timekeeping! He joined in well with the now familiar scraps from end to end in the limo. Loz had now progressed to bringing a toy gun that would propel plastic balls at an unacceptably unpleasant speed if they hit you or anyone else who got in the way. Our arrival at Wembley was well on time, at least three hours before kick off as stipulated by the Wembley ground safety officer. Barbara was in fine form on the reception area as was Trevor the security guard on the entrance door. We picked up our packed lunches as usual and sneaked Barbara a few bits for later before being lead to our seats. This would involve a walk through Wembley on whichever way our escort would choose. Marc Armstrong was our man early on, Marc was destined for higher things with the FA, later in his career being the

Commercial Manager but he started with us and again a genuine football fan even if it was Arsenal he supported. Our guys were always supposed to be on their best behaviour especially when being escorted to our seats so when we walked around the pitch and up to the stand I expected everyone to be behind me which they were, apart from Brian. 'Cast Iron' or just 'Cast' as we'd named him had decided that he couldn't walk past the Wembley dug out without taking the opportunity to sit in the Glenn Hoddle / Alf Ramsey seat. I delivered the deserved bollocking and he managed to climb his way up the stand to the very back row which is, and was, our preferred position at games. Poor old Brian got an awful lot of stick because he would bite at the slightest bit of bait that any of us put in front of him and we saw it as great sport. One such wind up would be to flick his hair up on top of his head. He had a mini 'comb over' going on which exposed a weakness to us of trying to hide a bit of receding. We also knew he had no idea who the group 'The Prodigy' were and even less idea about the song 'Firestarter'. We would flick his hair up to a peak and shout, 'I am the fire starter!' at him to which he would go mad specially after the fiftieth time on a long trip down south. Brain though was a very good player and settled in with the rest of us for the game when he finally did make it to the back of the stand.

There was a tension in the air by kick off time but the fans apprehension was soon eased when we got the first goal, the second goal and the third. Moldova were no match for us that night, the final score being 4-0 to England and Wembley was bouncing to our various terrace chants as was now becoming normal and a welcome fitting tribute to how much effort we'd all put in. Murray would often leave a game with his hands blistered and bleeding from the friction of the drum sticks and along with the rest of us would sweat cobs during the ninety minutes to the point where our clothes were ringing wet especially in the summer months. The Moldova game took place in September but it was a warm night, none of this matters when you've just won 4-0 though.

The Moldova game being now past, the big one was on the horizon, Italy, away in Rome. As anticipated all those months earlier because of both team's results the Rome game was now set up as the game that would determine who qualified automatically for the Word Cup in France the following year. Every England fan wanted to be at the game and all we needed to do was avoid defeat to go through to the World Cup finals.

The Sun had come up trumps again and sorted out our travel which meant that more of us could be at the game forming a bigger band able to create a better atmosphere than ever before. We did the obligatory photos for the Sun around the coliseum in Rome and again with the guys that dress up as gladiators for the tourists to pose with. Word came back from home that these photos were plastered over a double page spread in the next day's Sun. Quite a place Rome, I don't know what we expected but I remember being surprised at the number of Roman ruins there were all over the city. Maybe I'd expected them to be knocked down, how stupid not to think that Rome would be full of Roman ruins. We saw what is known as the type writer, climbed the Spanish Steps and saw the various famous fountains. We had to return to the Spanish steps for an interview with Ray Stubbs for Radio 5. Naturally they wanted a tune, this was radio, so we started to play only to be stopped by the local police who must have feared some kind of disorder. Next stop was the Mark and Lard show on Radio One, they were broadcasting from some old building in Rome that we found by taxi and a short interview later we were back in the taxis ready to go to the game.

Stories had reached us of various skirmishes between fans and worryingly of Italian fans riding round two on a scooter with the passengers wielding knives. One Leeds fan reportedly was stabbed as he walked down the footpath when a scooter rode past him. It was time to rely on that sixth sense that we had as football fans which means you become anonymous wherever you are, keep your head down and get to the game as quickly as possible. This isn't always easy when you're all dressed as England fans in Italy's capital city but we managed to find our way to the Olympic Stadium without coming to harm. Italians have a well documented sense of fashion and other England fans weren't as lucky as us obviously standing out too much.

It is normal to come across different cordons of security as you approach a stadium abroad especially because England were the opposition and the reputation of the fans from previous times went before them. We knew this was going to be the case for this game so arrived in good time. There were some 14,000 England fans in Rome for the game and the sensible ones were already in the stadium. It was chaos all around the stadium, nobody seemed to know where the England turnstiles were and there was precious little help coming from the Italian police. By default we found the correct turnstile, having had the instruments checked twice already by the police. We knew that we were able to gain access to the stadium with the instruments because the FA do a fantastic job of clearing the way for us in pre match meetings with the opposition for every away game and anyway Trevor Francis had told us that it was normal in Italy to have drums. This doesn't mean that things went smoothly because the Italian authorities had their own way of doing things. The final checkpoint before we entered the stadium was a full search. We were asked to stand to one side to await clearance from whoever needed to be asked as all the other fans were searched. What we witnessed wasn't good viewing as we waited. All England fans young or old, male or female had anything they had on them taken from them including all the coins from their pockets, lipsticks and perfume from women, lighters, pens, keys you name it. We witnessed things of particular value being put into unused police helmets placed on the ground near the search area. Nothing could be claimed back after the game, not a chance, not that that was ever offered as an option, it was so so wrong and very frustrating to watch knowing that we could do nothing about it.

We eventually got the clearance that allowed us to enter the stadium and found our preferred position, at the back of the open terrace stood on the plastic seats that were fixed to the concrete terracing. England had been allocated the side of the stadium with 7,000 fans in two columns each side of the media area, that overlooked the halfway line. The main body of Italian fans were to our left and already in full voice. What they didn't know was that we had a secret weapon up our sleeves that night that was to change the sound of all future England games and our lives a bit more as it happened.

Looking back many things added up for us that night. There was the game itself as the main ingredient that had been building up as the biggest game of the qualifying period for months, the fact that 14,000 fans were there, the way fans had to avoid trouble all day in the build up to the game, the appalling organisation around the stadium, the treatment by the police and what was tantamount to legalised theft of their belongings on entering the stadium all revved the fans up so much that they were really ready for this game and so were we. The band struck up on kick off as normal with the tunes that had become familiar to fans at home but the secret weapon was the introduction of 'The Great Escape', a tune that every Englishman knows, it's almost institutionalised in us all. The fans belted out the song in our section 7,000 strong and it wasn't long until the adjacent section of 7,000 joined in too.

Moments later seats started to be thrown from the Italian section into the English section which revved the fans up even more. We made sure that we were out of range of anything that was being thrown including seats that were on fire, as the game continued.

I can remember Sol Campbell playing the game of his life, he was absolutely outstanding that night, his opponent didn't get an inch and Ian Wright had a chance from which I am still willing the ball into the net even today, somehow it just managed to miss the goal.

England fans were rightly getting fed up with being bombarded with missiles from the Italian section. Remarkably Italian fans were able to run right up to the divide between the fans that was lined by police with whatever they were throwing, let it go and return with the next missile unchallenged by the police. Some England fans retaliated by throwing things back and were immediately set upon by batten wielding police. This caused a stampede in our section and a batten charge was in progress in the other England section too. This seemed to be the price for turning up to support our team, well it just spurred us on even more. We'd done nothing but support England as best we could along with every other England fan and we were going to out shout the Italians of Serie A big time. This is exactly what happened as the game progressed, Italy came close to scoring, Maldini in particular with a header just over the top. The Great Escape rang out as loud as could be imagined from 14,000 passionate fans and the Italians couldn't compete, they were defeated off the pitch. What drives us to do what we do is a belief that we can create that twelfth man off the field that encourages the performance on the pitch and when it all comes together it is awesome. Everything came together that night for all the Englishmen in the stadium, those on the pitch and those off it. It was the best 0-0 draw that I and many, if not all, the fans had ever seen and will probably ever see as long as they live. We had qualified for the World Cup on the Italians home patch and the Great Escape was debuted as a new

England song to trumpet the result and qualification, it didn't get better than that.

One thing that did happen that night I will remember for ever as a very proud and humbling experience. After the game had finished and we had celebrated with the crowd as the elated players came round the pitch to clap the fans thanking them for their support the fans turned round to face us at the back and started to applaud. The applause spread until all the fans in our section were facing us and applauding and cheering our efforts. We didn't really know what to do, we'd had compliments before but never something of this magnitude. To be recognised in this way by our fellow fans in such an impromptu manner added to the compliment they were paying us. It was so unusual and surreal too because these fans were die hard tough football fans as we were, proper blokes, these kind of things didn't go off on the terrace but it did that night. Of the eight of us there that night we were all humbled that is of course apart from Jimmy the student who was in a rock band and always wanted to be a pop star. When we looked at him he had his hands aloft milking the applause as if he was Mick Jagger or something. A few months later he was overheard telling people that we'd played Wembley and the Olympic Stadium as if he was a pop star. He got a bit mixed up and forgot that the fans actually come to watch the football, just as we do.

Little did we know what was to come after the game that night in Rome. The organisation was appalling or rather the lack of organisation and the police were no help at all. It is the norm now that away supporters are locked in the stadium after the game so that the home crowd can disperse making the release of the away fans easier to manage. The waiting period is usually fifteen maybe thirty minutes, not this time. We were held in the ground for almost three hours. I say ground because we were moved from the terrace to an area behind the stand with no lighting, no toilets and no refreshments. Above all there was no explanation as we waited to be released as to why we were being held. There were no other fans anywhere near the stadium especially after three hours and a serious situation developed particularly for the older people, women and children in the crowd. I can recall Bram being particularly uncomfortable sat on the floor with the rest of us for three hours.

When we did get out of the pen they'd put us in it was the early hours of the morning and there was no public transport running of any kind so a procession of England fans formed from the Olympic Stadium back to the city centre. I don't know how long the walk was but it seemed like miles. What made things worse was that we were all staying in different hotels for some reason. The best way of finding your hotel abroad and keeping safe is to get in a taxi and ask the driver to take you to your hotel, easy. We tried to hail a taxi, then another, then another, all of which were empty but to no avail. We were in full view of a police van full of Carbinari so we asked why the taxi's weren't stopping to be told they had been instructed not to stop for English fans. When we asked what we should do now they told us they couldn't help, then got in their van and left us.

As we neared the city centre it was clear that all was not well ahead of us. You develop a trained ear as one of your sixth sense football survival kit when you've been to as many matches as we have, i.e. a match every week for about forty years so far. The best course of action was to get Bram back to his hotel, after about an hour and a half's walk. Gradually we dropped off band members at their various hotels which left Murray and myself to find ours somewhere. Groups of Italian fans were roaming the streets in search of English fans so, a little worried, we looked up and down the streets for our hotel with no luck. The only answer was that we knew where Antonella from The Sun was staying so we went to that hotel booked in at about 4 a.m. as her and crashed in her room. Remarkably she wasn't in having also fallen victim to the same organisation afforded us and having to do her job as well. She did get a surprise when she came back in the room to find two hairy-arsed Yorkshiremen in her bed. We were just pleased to finally be safe and in a bed somewhere.

In the morning we awoke to find that we were indeed in the wrong hotel but were so ecstatic that we'd qualified we wouldn't have cared if we were on the moon. Quickly everybody else was rounded up from various parts of Rome for the trip to the airport and home. We had two flights to catch to get home one was to take us to Geneva where we would change and fly back home. We'd started to develop quite a routine when booking in at the airport in a fun way just because that's what we do. It usually involved getting to know the girl on the check-in desk and the guy in the outsized baggage. There is a bit of tactical manoeuvring going on as far are we're concerned because getting good seats and making sure your luggage gets to your destination, especially instruments, are very important. Our routine continues onto the plane and air crews are fair game and usually good fun after initially sussing out what we're like and that we're not drunk, a topic of much fun for us, especially with me not drinking and none of the others really being bothered either.

Once we've managed to board and settled into our seats we prepare for the safety briefing. A very serious operation not to be scoffed at but we've heard it so many times before that we know it off by heart and usually everyone travelling with us, mostly regular England fans, have heard it too. So when the poor girl doing the demonstration takes her position in the aisle and lifts the safety card into the air another eight or more are instantly thrust into the air from our group. This is the point when the stewardess loses it but unfortunately for her she has to continue and you may have guessed it, with every move we mimic and add sound effects. This is usually done a split second before they have to do it, so seat belts are repeatedly clicked before they are demonstrated, we whistle just before it is pointed out on the life jacket, there is a big blow of breath just before the top up tube and oxygen masks are announced and all the exits are pointed out moments before the stewardess does so. Many stewardesses have ended up in stitches before the end of the demonstration but never to the detriment of safety, never, oh no.

The flight back to Geneva was with Italia airways with a number of other nationalities on the plane. Our high jinx continued fuelled by the match result and we became a little boisterous, nothing too bad but we didn't bank on being sat in front of a German lady who took exception to our juvenile behaviour and uttered another phrase that has stayed with us, "Dis is not a Kintergarten!" We offered our apologies and sat like naughty schoolboys for the rest of the trip with the odd unstoppable chuckle bursting out when it couldn't be held anymore and yes, we're talking grown men here.

Chapter Six

The whole of England had gone World Cup mad! 'Three Lions on the shirt!' All that was going on following Skinner and Baddiel's 1996 wonder hit. We were blissfully unaware at the time but when we were in Rome for "the best nil nil draw ever" i.e. the game that clinched qualification to France '98, there were two record producers in the crowd witnessing the birth of the Great Escape as a terrace song. On our return to England I was to get a call from East West records and V2 both asking if we were interested in making a World Cup single. Both companies wanted to release the Great Escape as theirs and our World Cup single. I phoned Murray up to let him know and that eternal phrase came out, "This is f******g ridiculous!" I couldn't argue it was ridiculous but it was about to get even dafter.

We didn't know the first thing about records or record deals and we'd heard all the stories about the Music Industry being full of sharks so I turned to Martin Ware for a bit of advice as the only person I really knew who'd had dealings with record companies and we'd done the Wednesday record together and become good friends so he was a big help. Martyne had a lot of success with Heaven 17 in the 80's and produced records for many other artists so was a big help when the two companies started to persuade us to sign with them.

Trying to keep our feet firmly on the ground we went to London for meetings with both companies and ended up more or less with the same offer. We'd still no idea what we were talking about but we'd got the promise of a video and so many points which we found out later to be the percentage that you get after costs, etc., as far as records deals are concerned.

At V2, which was the Virgin groups record label, they had made a special effort by kitting out all their staff in Wednesday home and away shirts when we went down for the meeting with them. So when we walked into their reception the three receptionists had our kit on and in the office there were about twenty of them. Even the lunch menu had Carboni pasta and Di Canio sauce, both Wednesday players at the time so they were really trying. Despite all of this we managed to keep our wit's about us and left to consider what we should do next back on the train to Sheffield first class. I mention first class because we saw a banker friend of ours on the railway platform who travelled regularly to London with work. He took great delight in telling us that we were at the wrong end of the platform for when the train arrived because second class was towards the back end of the train so we'd need to be further down the platform. Oh, how we slaughtered him all the way home, much to his embarrassment in front of his banking colleagues. Just the odd shout every 10 or 15 minutes to make sure he was OK and to get more advice on where to get a coffee or anything else we could think of. Well, he was the expert, wasn't he?

The next day I was back to work at the car and van rental franchise in Wakefield. I had to go to Doncaster to collect a car and when I got there the large mobile phone rang and a voice said, "Is that John?" I said, "Yes," because it was me and the lady explained that she was from Virgin and I would be getting a call from the owner of the company in the next few minutes. The next thing the phones rings and it's Richard Branson! "Hello John, this is Richard Branson............."

I can't remember word for word what was said but Richard (what else could I call him) assured us that he was right behind V2's bid to sign us and if there was anything else he could do to let him know. He even said that if we were down in London give him a call and we could do lunch. I still have his mobile number to this day. What do you say after that call? I gave Murray a ring and you can guess what he said. "This is f******* ridiculous!" That kind of thing doesn't happen every day and that was enough to persuade us that V2 would be the company to sign with. Personal call from Richard Branson, (Dicky B as he affectionately became known) what else could we do?

As soon as the press found out about the Branson call and the record deal the phone started to go mad again. This time it was TV and radio appearances with Big Breakfast and the Richard and Judy Show asking us to appear. It was great fun for all the lads and lass in the band but it didn't do much for renting cars and vans and the business inevitably took a bit of a hit. I was enjoying it all the same despite the clear financial downside, we were all loving it and the video was next.

The next thing we had to do was to make a video for the record that was to be 'The Great Escape' by The England Supporters Band. The idea for the video was to centre on London City airport with a couple of celebrities included, those being ex-England internationals, Paul Walsh and Clive Allen. Great players but they really pulled out all the stops when they got 1966 World Cup hero, Geoff Hurst to appear in the video supposedly riding a Steve McQueen style motor bike and revealing his identity at the last minute. We were trying to remain cool but also realising that we had best get his autograph before the end of filming. Adolf had quite a starring role doing keepy-uppy, in fact we all played our part at different times and the resulting video was quite good.

The film crew had dressed us in some rather nice England branded gear for the shoot and most of the extras as well so there was a bag of goodies lying around on the airport concourse when we finally finished shooting after midnight. Somehow that bag managed to find its way into our car via a combination of Loz and Murray skulduggery and one of the most memorable band moments was to occur at Toddington Services on the M1 near Luton on the way home. That was the distribution of the loot. We felt safe there as it's our most used service station stopping there after every game right to this day to see Pete and Linda and previously, Helen, who we understand isn't so well at the moment.

All the items were spread out on the tables of the self-service restaurant, at which point we all realised that there was a limited amount of decent stuff and the rest was, well crap as far as a football fan was concerned. The prize asset was a long England branded coat that everyone had their eye on. The thing was that it was massive! We'd decided the pecking order and systematically each member of the band tried unsuccessfully to convince us that the coat fitted them. The most comical being Murray who is one of the shortest in the band and a lot slimmer then than he is now. Watching him trying to grow another six inches in height and in the arms at the same time had us all in stitches especially when at the same time it was accompanied by a rant about how it actually did fit him and we didn't know what we were talking about. Inevitably he had to pass it down the line and settle for a hi-vis vest that said, 'Air Traffic Control' on the back. The most bizarre thing that happened was that half way through the distribution of the clothing Nick Barmby and some policemen walked into the restaurant and we quickly hid all the stuff like he was going to grass us up and they were going to confiscate the stuff or something. What he was doing there after midnight was anybody's guess. We were to come across Paul Walsh, Clive Allen and Geoff Hurst later on this roller coaster ride that is the England Band.

So our first record was produced courtesy of Richard Branson and his V2 label. The record wasn't bad, it sounded nothing like us though by the time they'd finished mixing it in the studio which wasn't necessarily a bad thing. The reality was that it sounded a lot better than we did. If you've ever heard us you'll know exactly what I mean. We're not something that you would choose to listen to for entertainment which is where so many critics get us wrong. We're not entertainment at all really, not in the true sense but what we are is one of the best groups of atmosphere generators in the country if not the world. Through sheer enthusiasm, volume, experience and knowledge of football crowds and songs, not forgetting considerable pride and passion, we manage to generate an atmosphere that players and fans can thrive on in the joint belief that what we are all doing together will help us beat the opposition.

Generally speaking, with England, we have enjoyed a fair percentage of wins match-wise but no trophies yet. At Sheffield Wednesday we haven't been so successful but, it could be argued that we'd probably have lost more than we actually had if we'd not been there. Does it work then? Well, whenever we've spoken to players we've taken the opportunity to ask them if they think having the band and more vocal support helps them on the pitch and even allowing for the fact that they are bound to give the answer of yes, when pressed they confirm definitely that it helps. Peter Atherton, the captain of Sheffield Wednesday, in the late nineties, confirmed this with evidence of a game away at Chelsea when we were two nil down and the players fought for ninety minutes inspired by the crowd, lead by the band with the equalising goal coming in the last minute of injury time. He insisted that if the fans had given up then they would have too but because we kept going the inspiration was there for the players to carry on. Some of the best compliments we've had have been from opposition managers like Neil Warnock and Peter Reid who have both complimented us as being a plus factor for the opposition when they played against us.

So the video was shot, the record produced and launch day approached. We sort of kept it quiet in Sheffield not wanting to sound like we were getting too big for our boots, these things matter on the terraces or maybe we thought they did more than they actually did but for whatever reason we kept it quiet locally whilst the record company was shouting loudly nationally.

What we didn't realise was how big the England fan base is, a little naive really because it's, basically, every football fan that is English, in fact, it's more than that at tournament time because everyone seems to be interested in football when it's the World Cup. Dare I say it, even women, and that's said with the utmost respect to the vast numbers of female football fans out there who I'm sure know what I mean.

The record was launched and we did a personal appearance at the Virgin Record store on Oxford Street. We were collected in a fleet of seven seater vehicles and delivered to the back door in true pop star fashion. Nobody knew how many people would be in the store waiting for us and thats exactly who were there..............nobody! Apart from those who were in there shopping anyway that is but we soon managed to get rid of those few by playing in our normal style.

It was great though to see our CD on the shelves of all the record shops and every member of the band went into a record shop at some time to buy our own record just for the experience, again you can't do that every week. There were a few good football records released at the time, Fat Les and his Vindaloo song, Dario G's Parc de Paris but the one that made the number one spot was a re-release of Skinner and Baddeil's Three Lions with a '98 World Cup version. Three Lions is quite clearly the best football record ever produced in no short measure and we put this down to the fact that genuine football fans, Skinner and Baddiel, were involved with quality musicians. We had slight issues with the other two in that in our opinion we had made the Fat Les and Dario G tunes known to the footballing public from the terraces. We were told that Dario G credited us with making it popular which is nice but it would have been nicer to have got some of the funds to help us travel and support the team. Fat Les (Keith Allen) was a bit different again in our opinion, he had just taken our song and changed a few notes and milked it. We were later to bump into him in France whilst on a Radio One interview which proved a very interesting confrontation.

There was clearly a lot of competition and high quality at that so V2 (the record company) gambled and released the record later than they normally would. Was this the beginning or the end of our chart career?

Chapter Seven

World Cup fever had taken over England in the build up to France '98 and we, along with everyone else, were sure that this was the year that we would win. The media were building up the expectation and The Sun had recruited us to add to the World Cup publicity in exchange for help with our travel costs. This suited us because without their help we'd have to find the money ourselves and some of the lads simply couldn't afford it. All we had to do was pose for a few photos and give quotes which were good fun in themselves.

The football pre World Cup revolved around friendly games at home and away. Four games at Wembley interspersed by an away game against Switzerland. Cameroon, Chile, Portugal and Saudi Arabia were the opposition at Wembley where we were managing to establish ourselves with the full backing of the fans and Wembley was getting noisier. That is apart from the Saudi Arabia game. Our instructions for Wembley games at the time were to report three hours prior to kick off and gain access via the staff gate and someone would guide us to our seats. For the Saudi Arabia game, Max, one of our drummers, was running late and arrived at the top of Wembley Way bang on three hours before kick off. This meant that we arrived at our meeting point a minute late. Unfortunately that minute was one too late for the safety officer in charge at the time who refused us entry. We were told that we could enter without our instruments and sit in the same seats but not with instruments. We were devastated, it's a long way from Sheffield with a day off work and your heart set on playing to be told it's not happening. I was absolutely hopping mad with Max but we'd learned another lesson about safety officers, they are a breed amongst themselves. At the end of the day if we'd been there a minute earlier we'd have got in without a problem but we thought it harsh, to say the least. There was no way that it was ever going to happen again.

A new snare drummer had joined the band for two of the friendly games by the name of Helen Chamberlain from Sky's Soccer AM show. We were extremely pleased to have Helen in our ranks but the amount of attention she attracted from autograph hunters in the stands at Wembley meant that it was impossible for her to play or watch the game. Very unfortunately Helen had to stop playing with us but we were to keep in touch via Soccer AM appearances and other events.

The band were taken to Morocco courtesy of The Sun for the pre World Cup tournament between England, Belgium and Morocco and a couple of publicity stunts took place to promote the record and The Sun's support.

We had recruited an adviser, Adam Black (a Man City fan which made him OK), who was to help us try and get some sponsorship to help fund the World Cup trips and beyond. We had a bit of success with free products, in particular we ended up with free Doctor Martin boots and an England mobile phone which were quite cool but didn't really help us in what we needed which was some way of paying for the trips ahead. Not that we were ungrateful but we didn't really know what we were doing either.

Adam took us to the Doctor Marten's shop in Covent Garden to pick a pair of boots each and this was to be the start of the publicity stunt that was a march from Covent Garden to Trafalgar Square with a couple of Sun page three models. The models were Cathy Lloyd and a relatively new model called Jordan, who held the two St. George cross flags aloft in front of us on the march. We did the march playing all the way including dodging a water bomb thrown out of one of the office windows, that we took personally.

The Morocco trip was to turn out to be very memorable. We went to Morocco for about four days and the incidents started as soon as we arrived. Such is the reputation of England fans abroad you can always bank on a reception from the local army or armed police force as a minimum, if indeed, you can tell the difference. Morocco was no exception even if a little surprising when there were only one hundred and fifty-eight England fans travelling. Heavily armed guards were everywhere at the airport. As we got off the plane and entered the airport building soldiers were lined up shoulder to shoulder each bearing a machine gun and all looking at the group of Englishmen that had just arrived. It was red hot and the airport authorities had provided a stall stacked high with bottles of water in a pyramid formation, a very welcome site to us all. That was until Loz inadvertently bumped into the stall as he walked past nudging it enough to bring the whole lot crashing down to the floor. Immediately that this happened the rifles were cocked and pointing at Loz, who I've never seen move so fast picking up as many as possible and putting them back on the stall. At this stage we're thinking he's going to get arrested and we've not even made it through customs yet!

We did make it through customs and to the hotel. The usual ritual of claiming that you had the best room took place before we assembled for the photos that we had to produce for The Sun. Antonella Lazzerri was the Sun reporter that accompanied us with the 'snapper'. They had us dressed in fezzes and the long dress gear that the Moroccan's wear and took some photos on the beach where there were no sunbathers, this being a Muslim country. After the photos we were travelling back to the hotel when we came across a crowd in a back street. On closer inspection we could see that they were watching a football match. We stopped the bus and went to investigate with a view to giving them a tune for a bit of fun. It turned out that the game was taking place at the side of another, more organised, game on a sandy pitch next door.

Not being shy we asked if we could play them, England v Morocco, street style. The offer was accepted with Murray, Adolf, Jimmy, Max, Loz (keeper) and I forming the team and Bram and Brian providing the music. As we played the crowd got bigger and bigger until we were totally surrounded by a crowd about four or five deep on all sides and no-one was watching the other game. So much so that the local crowd control man turned up with his unique method of controlling them and keeping them off the pitch. This was by whacking them with a stick with a couple of nails hammered through the end whenever they encroached on to the pitch - extremely crude but affective. By the time we'd finished there were hundreds watching this street game that ended 2-2 and all singing the Great Escape in a big group after the match. A drawn game but great victory for international relations.

The England games in the tournament were to take place on consecutive days with Morocco first. Loz had been under instruction from his wife to cover up due to scares of skin cancer, so he'd been dispatched with sun block and persuaded to use it. We didn't expect to see Casper the Ghost though when we assembled for the game! He'd covered himself in white sun block and if he'd painted his face in white emulsion he wouldn't have looked any whiter! He has remained 'Casper' ever since when the subject of sun is raised. What topped it off was that when we entered the Mohammed V stadium, which is massive, the terracing was completely open all the way around with the exception of a small section adjacent to the halfway line measuring fifty yards or so. This was the area designated to the England fans so Casper was sat in the shade anyway, much to the amusement of us all!

A special affection existed between us and the England physiotherapist, Alan Smith, acknowledged by a routine that we performed at Wembley and all games abroad whenever we saw him. Alan was our club physio in addition to being the England physio and a great bloke so we'd play his tune and sing his name as he trotted round the pitch before the games, waiting for the acknowledgement of a wave that came every time. He did look surprised when this happened amidst the hustle and noise of fifty-eight thousand Moroccan fans swaying around three hours before kick off.

The actual games were very drab affairs with England beating Morocco 1-0 and drawing 0-0 in front of next to nobody the following day.

This left us with a day and night at leisure. In that twenty four hour period Brian managed to get mugged in the bazaar, claiming to have had £500 pounds stolen when we've never known him to have any money on him ever. In the evening at the hotel karaoke night we ended up stood on chairs singing in a very high pitch about Mexico and a man dressed in a linen suit. Another highlight of the karaoke was when we'd taken over the resident bands instruments and had our go at singing and Brian stepped up to sing 'My way.' Unbeknown to Brian, Murray had acquired another microphone, so when he started singing, Murray was under the table repeating everything he sang with a few choice words added for comfort.

Better was to come later in the hotel basement night club. After managing to gain entry in shorts, which was against the rules, we found that the place was full of women. Having noticed that there weren't any women elsewhere in the bars this was immediately quite a pleasant surprise. Those of us a little more worldly-wise and sober quickly realised what was going on, however, our two young student boys, Max and Jimmy, revelled in the fact that they'd managed to 'pull' two rather better looking girls than they perhaps would have normally. Jimmy in typical style invited the girl upstairs to his room where she promptly asked for payment, much to his shock and disgust. He threw her out of his room when he realised that she didn't really love him, but that wasn't the end. The girl had to get past reception but they were clearly on a cut of any money earned for turning a blind eye as girls accompanied guests to their rooms. We were called to reception due to the almighty row that was going on between the girl and the porter who didn't believe that no payment had been made from Jimmy. A few valuable lessons were learned on this trip.

The build up to the World Cup was complete and we were about to get an unbelievable offer. I got a phone call from Antonella, from The Sun, saying they were very happy with what we'd done and how would we like it if they took us to France but we had to spend two weeks with the top page three model, Melinda Messenger, and do some publicity on an open top bus. Well, I then had to make the call to the lads. "How do you fancy going to France for the World Cup? You haven't got to find as much money as you thought and you've got to spend it with Melinda Messenger." You can imagine what Murray and I said, "This is f****** ridiculous!"

Needless to say the rest of the lads and lass couldn't believe it.

Chapter Eight

The build up to France '98 was in full flow with the nation's expectations higher than ever. St. George's cross flags started to appear all over the place, not just up flag poles but in windows, shops, trucks and almost every car on a plastic pole attached to the window. These became strewn all over England due to people forgetting they had them and winding the window down.

It was an unbelievable offer from The Sun, taking us over to France and spending time with Melinda Messenger and everyone in the band thought I was joking, but they soon realised that it was for real when we were asked to have a photo shoot in London with Melinda. So, we turned up in London, very excited, for the photo shoot and were put up in a hotel in Docklands. There had developed a bit of a tradition of messing around in various hotels that we stayed in but the overriding rule, that still applies today, is that there will never be irreparable damage. This is a strict rule as respect for other people's property is paramount.

Murray and I roomed together as usual and next door were Loz, Max and Jimmy with a video camera. I somehow found myself in their room when we arrived which always puts the others on guard as phones, clothes, toiletries, anything can go missing. Maybe by way of trying to distract me from doing something in their room Loz proposed a plan to attack Murray who was next door. This would involve me going back into our room and putting a piece of paper between the door and the frame where the door lock is. This would allow access for the three of them to come in and raid our room, attacking Murray in the process.

I agreed to the plan and went back to our room with a smile on my face. To make the plan successful I would have to double cross my roommate and take a hit myself when they raided the room. This was never going to happen but Loz and his team didn't know that. They filmed their preparation which involved mixing deep heat and crisps in their hands ready to smear on Murray and included detailed pledges of exactly what they were going to do to him when they'd got him pinned down.

When I went into our room I placed the paper in the door that allowed access from outside and promptly set about telling Murray of their plan and hatching our own counter plan. Murray was in bed so he got up in his underpants, I was ready for bed too when we decided to fill the room's waste bin and the kettle with water and hide in the wardrobe. The wardrobe was one of those sliding door jobs that you get in hotels just inside the door and so perfectly placed for when they were to dive into the room because they'd go right past us and be trapped. We dimmed the lights and the old trick of putting pillows in the beds to look as if we were asleep.

So there we were, two grown men, semi-naked inside the wardrobe, one with a bucket full of water and one with a kettle full of water, with no lid, waiting in anticipation for the raid. Now if room service had called what would they have made of that, not only would they have seen two semi-naked men emerge from the wardrobe but they'd have got covered in water into the bargain!

As it was, our rivals video'd the approach to the room down the corridor and expressed their delight when they saw the piece of paper sticking out of the door. Inside it seemed like ages, at least 20 minutes, waiting inside the wardrobe for them to come. I cannot begin to explain the hysteria and laughter inside that wardrobe as we lay in wait for them. The anticipation was unbearable and the various false alarms that occurred when we heard the slightest noise only added to the madness of the situation. We were absolutely killing ourselves laughing and if anything was f****** ridiculous it was this.

In a flash the door to our room was flung open to a cry of, "Get the bastards!" Jimmy flew past us in the wardrobe onto the bed and attacked the pillow in Murray's bed smearing it with deep heat and crisps as he'd promised, closely followed by Max and Loz who jumped on the other bed beating the pillow that they thought was me. Almost simultaneously Murray and I emerged from the wardrobe in our underpants and drenched the three of them from head to foot giving them a good kicking as they tried to exit as fast as they came in. The looks of surprise as we came out of the wardrobe had to be seen to be believed and the laughter afterwards on top of the 20 minutes inside the wardrobe well............ We still laugh at that now and that set the bar for room raids.

Cars picked us up from the hotel the next day which was a first and off we went to the studio for the photo shoot. We met Melinda for the first time and her boyfriend/manager Wayne who took the ogling of Melinda very well it has to be said. We found out that he met Melinda on a blind date because he didn't have a partner for a college dance that he had to go to. Some blind date that one!

The photos were great and were published in the next day's paper. It has to be said that Mellinda was fabulous with us and fantastic company and so our stay together in France went well. I'm not sure what Julie, our only female member thought of it but we were loving it.

A film production company had contacted us on behalf of Channel 4's Cutting Edge programme to see if they could film the band in France and at home in the build up to France'98. Cutting Edge! It rang a few warning bells but we met the guy, 'Rupert' and decided to go ahead. We knew the type of programmes that Cutting Edge made which by definition had an edge to them. Our guard was up because we also knew that if a TV crew get enough film they can almost create situations and portray a story that isn't really there.

The filming was to take place at each band member's home and I recall getting it in the ear from my girlfriend at the time who wasn't too keen on any film crew entering the house and was the only one associated with the band to refuse to be interviewed by them. So it was and filming took place with everyone else before we left. And, the crew were to follow us in France.

One recent addition to the band at this time was a mate of ours called Tino who joined to enhance the drum section or actually, we needed a drummer and asked our mate if he'd do it. He couldn't believe his luck of course, World Cup, England, Melinda and all that. He knew the crack as well so fitted in quite well. He's also a bit of a lad - certain incidents with young ladies can't be written about, unfortunately. Suffice to say, Tino had a very good time and a great laugh in France.

The Band had picked up a deal with the kit manufacturer, Admiral, who supplied us with England branded clothing to be worn at the games, so we'd all looked the part when the day arrived to leave for France from Heathrow airport. Important to say though that we didn't look like we were going to our first game, football fashion is important to proper football fans.

The check-in staff got the usual treatment at Heathrow as did the cabin crew on the flight to Nice via Charles de Gaule, all filmed for Cutting Edge. Rupert was the producer and camera man and took considerable stick for being from the south and being called Rupert which was always going to be enough for us to slaughter him at every opportunity. He wasn't a bad lad really but his mate, Charlie, who helped him occasionally, had the smelliest feet ever, worse than stinking bishop!

Another appearance in front of the camera prior to leaving was on GMTV with Ant and Dec and Sharron Davison when we met Luther van Dross. Ant and Dec understood us and our sense of humour straight away and could easily have joined the band with their genuine football fan background and banter to suit. Luther asked us for directions when he arrived so we gave them freely and added that when he got there they'd give him a badge so that people would know who he is. Or, was he Alexander O'Neil? I'm still not sure.

So, we boarded the plane as excited as a bunch of school kids on their first trip out, our first World Cup, all lads together except Julie of course, our female member, South of France, Melinda Messenger and a single poised to enter the charts. Despite all of this our focus above anything else was to support the team through to the final and bring the World Cup back to England for the first time since 1966. Our feet were firmly on the ground even though we were enjoying ourselves - when you grew up where we did that's how it was.

When we arrived in Nice we met Antonella from The Sun who was brilliant - a few photos and off to the hotel. There was, however, one massive problem, Julie's trombone hadn't arrived and the game was the next day. We learned a valuable lesson that has haunted us on numerous occasions since which is that, if you have a change of flight, nine times out of ten your luggage will go missing and when it contains essential stuff, like instruments, we're in trouble.

Word went around about the missing trombone, Julie was quite upset having looked forward to playing for months and then at the last minute, disaster. The lost luggage people did their usual trying to find it but when it's a question of national pride and helping the England team the French officials didn't seem to be as bothered as we were and the word was that the trombone would hopefully be put on a flight and arrive in the next couple of days. Rubbish! That was no good, the game was the next day but what could we do? We just crossed our fingers and hoped for the best.

We had taxis to take us to the hotel and the race was then on to get the best rooms and into the pool as soon as possible. Murray and I roomed together as usual and dived into the room in an attempt to get the best bed, he's always on the left and me on the right but that doesn't stop us going through the ritual of diving in the room and on to the bed to claim it every time we enter a room.

Murray decided to look out of the window to see if the other guys had arrived at the pool, so, standing on the luggage rack, he peered out, saw them, made the obligatory moony only to then fall straight through the latts of the luggage rack to the sound of an almighty crack. Shit! We'd only been there a minute and managed to bust something. He went into the bathroom and I heard another crack. God knows how he'd managed it but he'd fallen on to the toilet system knocked the top off and it had broken in two. We sort of put it back together and pressed as if it would fuse together somehow, which it didn't, of course, but it made us feel better. This is us with a policy of no irreparable damage two minutes into the trip.

Into the pool we went and we'd managed to get a full size blow-up sofa from Tango that entered the pool with us. The Tango manufacturers were somehow associated with The Sun for the trip. Try as we might we couldn't get all of us onto it, or pop it, but much fun was had by all. Head tennis was next on the hotel tennis court; ultra competitive as we are this became as important as the World Cup itself (well not really). The ball went over the fence behind us off my foot, uncharacteristically might I add, and I felt duty bound to fetch it. Like Spiderman I dived on the wire fence to climb over and get the ball. The fence was about ten feet high and with my weight on it as I got nearer the top it started to curl over the top of me, the higher I went the more it curled until I was hanging upside down above some rose bushes still being pulled downwards and I was well and truly stuck. I couldn't go up because that was down and if a let go I'd end up falling and landing in the rose bushes which I didn't fancy. Never mind, one of the lads would rescue me. Not a chance, they were too busy pissing themselves with laughter and enjoying it to stop it happening. In the end I timed my fall to minimise the damage but the rose thorns did their job, much to the amusement of everyone else. They could fetch their own ball in future!

Duty called and we had to sing for our supper, so we had to meet the Sun open-top bus in Marseilles harbour and Melinda of course. No problem getting everyone motivated then and when we arrived at the bus there was the guy from the Tango advert too shouting down a megaphone. (Not the orange guy or our mate Paul from Sheffield Wednesday) but the one in the suit, who didn't go down that well in France, whereas Melinda had universal appeal. We hosted a few fans on the bus including our old friend, Graham Kelly, who we didn't really know that well but we'd played for V2 (the record label) against and FA team in London a few weeks before and football, being the great leveller, meant that we got on well. I think he and his wife were glad of the place to hide on the lower deck, out of the way of strolling England fans.

It was decided that the bus should start up and take us around Marseille to a beach where there was a big screen so that those who hadn't managed to get tickets could watch the first of the group games against Tunisia. The band were on the top deck and any England fans that we saw got a blast of whichever tune came into our heads. On arrival at the beach we found hundreds of England fans checking things out and a bit of a fan park that we parked next to and started playing. From nowhere a Brazilian samba band appeared and struck up next to the bus which we saw as competition so blasted them out of the water in our unique style. It all ended up very friendly though when the Brazilian dancers arrived and it seemed a much better idea to play a samba version of the Great Escape and so it was.

It was red hot and we were very grateful for the endless supply of Tango from the fridges on the lower deck. The majority of the fans were in bars around the harbour in Marseilles so when the bus went past with us playing on top it went down a treat leaving the fans in full voice before we left to the hotel for the day. When we got to the hotel we were just beginning to chill out when Antonella got a call from The Sun's offices saying that there was some trouble down by the harbour. She was on what she called hooli watch which was basically being ready to report and get on the scene if there was any bother caused by the fans.

She asked if we would drive her down so we did and when we arrived we found that there was some bother. Apparently some of the city's Tunisian population had decided to attack the England fans in the bar that we drove past earlier. When we arrived it was still happening but the police had intervened and most of the Tunisians had dispersed. That left tear-gas-firing police and the England fans. We dropped Antonella off and Murray and I set off back to the hotel. We were in a queue of traffic and every car in the queue was being rocked from side to side to try and turn them over. All too soon it became our turn but fortunately we had our England shirts on which spared us from the ordeal and saved any excess payment that may have resulted on the hire car.

The harbour was again the venue that night for a meal in a Mexican restaurant which seemed like a great idea fajitas and a live band, great. All of us crammed into the restaurant, Melinda, Wayne, Antonella, the eight of us from the band plus the bus crew and others that were there like Chris, who was the inner part of World Cup Willy, the mascot that the Sun had sent out. The innards of World Cup Willy is not a job you want when it is 85 degrees all day, so he was looking forward to a good night rehydrating.

The meal was great and much to our surprise when the tables were cleared the locals started to get on to the tables, encouraged by the waiters, to dance to the Mexican band at the far end of the room. It wasn't long before we were the only ones who weren't on the tables dancing, so, when in Rome we thought and it would've been rude not to, so, up we got onto the substantial tables that could easily stand our weight. Everyone was up and gigging around enjoying themselves and taking advantage of the rare opportunity to dance the night away on a table top. Everyone that was except for our oldest member, Bram.

Bram is a character that we cannot speak of highly enough. Having joined the band in its early stages Bram was an ever-present at Sheffield Wednesday and England games and a stalwart of the band. Bram's family, we were told, were very surprised that he'd joined us as he'd spent his working life in the bank when bank managers were very staid and prim and proper. Bram was also in the navy during the 1940's and we are proud to have an ex-serviceman in our ranks and he is a very welcome member of the band. Maybe, in his retirement, he has finally let go and enjoys his involvement, usually laughing at the rest of us.

Now, because of his age, being born in the 1920's (exactly when he keeps private) he understandably doesn't join in with all the antics and dancing on tables was one of those that falls into the category of 'perhaps its youngsters only'. That was until the end of the night when Bram decided that he should perhaps make an effort to get up onto the table for a dance. He got up there and all was well with him joining into the spirit of things until the fall. Bram was in fact dancing on two tables, one foot on each and the tables had started to move apart. Now Loz and World Cup Willy (Chris) were sat next to the two tables as the gap between them mysteriously grew wider. Bram suspects skulduggery and it wouldn't be beyond the realms of possibility although nobody would accept responsibility as Bram tumbled to the floor with one leg still on the table. Oh dear! You could see that it had hurt but Bram's biggest concern was that we didn't make a point of telling any of his family, especially his lovely wife, Barbara, who did (and still does) a wonderful job of looking after him. Let's face it none of us like to have a lecture from our other halves especially when we know they're right.

That wasn't the end of it though, as we quickly found out, if you knock around with the Sun things get reported. The journos from TV and the press tend to mix with each other too and so it was that word came back to us that on that night's News at Ten Trevor McDonald reported an injury to the England squad but not the team, it was Bram from the band who had injured his knee in the fall. We've not been told the full story about happenings on Bram's return home however, Bram did eventually end up having a plastic knee fitted such was the damage.

We slept well that night even with the excitement of the match looming the next day. Continental breakfast, never the same as an English, and off to the bus to do our bit before making our way very early to the stadium home of Marseilles. There were a lot of England fans around the stadium when we met our old friends the samba band and the dancers as we contributed to the pre match atmosphere by playing the odd tune or two. As soon as we strike up at games there's a TV crew who comes running to get the pictures of us and the fans singing along together and at a World Cup these cameras can belong to any country you can imagine. Honduras and Mexico were amongst them but then running through the crowd came an English camera crew that we recognised as the GMTV crew we'd been with earlier. The presenter was wielding a trombone and shouting at the top of his voice, "we've got you one!" All credit to GMTV they'd found us a trombone from somewhere, they'd actually hired it from a place in town which was just fantastic. Julie could now join in with us and be part of everything again. We felt for her because a musician without an instrument is like a singer losing their voice and in Julie's case not being able to support England to the full would have been devastating for her.

Fully equipped we made our way to the turnstiles which is always a trying time for us because we know we're going to meet stadium security. France '98 was to be no exception and the Gendarmerie stopped us to inspect what we had with us and announced that trumpets, trombones, saxophone, euphonium and drums were alright to go through but we weren't allowed any sticks to bang the drum with. The sticks we use are hammer headed and obviously we weren't going to use them for anything else other than banging the drum and what damage could they do that a trumpet couldn't? You get to the stage where you don't bother too much arguing because most security people revel in the authority invested in them so we agreed to enter as they had asked. Mysteriously the drum sticks turned up inside and nobody was hurt or injured in the making of atmosphere in support of the team.

As we approached the turnstile in the red hot sun it was becoming quite a squeeze as too many people through one turnstile doesn't go so we became quite well acquainted with our closest fellow fans. It was then that we got to the turnstile with the help of one confident fella who was shouting to the other fans, "watch out, band coming through, band coming through!" We all recognised the voice and we were right it was Emlyn Hughes, one of the all time England greats and great to see him entering the stadium with everyone else to support the team. He might not have realised but we appreciated his help and the banter about Sheffield, where he also lived, as we neared the turnstile.

So we'd made it into the ground, the Stade Velodrome and it is what it says on the tin, a big open stadium apart from one side that had a stand with a small roof. There were supposed to be 10,000 England fans with tickets for the match with about 50,000 applying and even more that would have liked to be there if they could. As the stadium filled up it was clear that there were going to be far more than 10,000 England fans in the stadium, it was nearer 30,000 England fans. Never underestimate the ability of football fans to obtain a ticket for a match by whatever means possible, this is always the case when England travel abroad, we are simply the best supported team in any tournament that we take part in, often having better support than the home nation.

There was a small pocket of Tunisian fans in one stand and the rest was England or neutral. The atmosphere was electric and there was an air of 'England expects'. Our sound was lost a little due to the open terrace but still enough to get the whole place bouncing with sound as the teams came out led by captain, Alan Shearer.

We were going hell for leather, this was it! The World Cup! England! Your country needs you! The crowd responded and we were off. The team started a little cautiously at first probably as a result of the level of expectation but soon got into their stride and Shearer rose just before half time to head us in front 1-0 England. It began to be party time even though at 1-0 there's always that chance of becoming too cocky and getting caught out but the team were delivering and although it took most of the second half, the second goal did come, from Paul Scholes a couple of minutes from the end of the game.

Brilliant! First game, first win and a clean sheet to match. Glenn Hoddle's army strode forth towards the next game v Romania in Toulouse.

Chapter Nine

The record company had been on the phone and reported that sales for the record were going well following the victory against Tunisia with all the major stores selling well and pre-ordering for the following week after our next game against Romania. We'd already made it into the top 30 according to Melody Maker and we'd all taken photos of the chart on teletext featuring us. It was one of those weird moments seeing ourselves in the charts and the record company were telling us that it would go top ten the following week so the excitement was almost unbearable. The world of records and the music business was a very strange one and completely alien to us. There's no wonder some artists complain about getting ripped off because even though we'd class ourselves as reasonably intelligent and V2 were great to work with, we'd no idea what was going on half the time.

So it was that we arrived in Toulouse for the our next game v Romania with The Sun helping us out with travel and Melinda and the open top bus all in toe. Same routine, dive in the bedroom, grab the bed and then off to the pool or beach. Tino was first ready, as keen as mustard in his flip flops and swimwear, towel round his neck, so we asked him to nip down to reception to get directions to the beach but to make an effort and ask the receptionist in French then she'd probably be more likely to help.

We managed to sneak down the stairs and hide just round the corner from reception but within earshot to hear Tino deliver the lines, "Bonjour madame. Ou est la plage?" The receptionist looked at his half naked beach prepared body and said, "Son ne pas la plage monsieur". Again Tino tried, "Ou est la plage?" and again the receptionist retorted, "Son ne pas le plage monsieur". This time with raised voice, Tino said, "Non, ou est la plage?" complete with swimming actions. We were pissing ourselves with laughter around the corner at the stand-off between the two. The receptionist clearly thought he was a complete idiot, it was like going down to reception in a Manchester hotel and asking where the beach was. Anyone with the slightest geographical knowledge of France would know that Toulouse isn't on the coast, the sea being some considerable distance away but not Tino. He heard us laughing from around the corner and following his enlightenment promised that he'd get us back in between a barrage of foul language. We took our positions by the hotel pool still laughing. A legendary moment, "Ou est la plage".

The next game of the tournament against Romania was probably the hardest game of the group with Romania having quite a good side, containing some recognised players of note. Petrescu, Popescu and Hagi to name a few. We were well capable of beating them and from our point of view we were determined to give it our all in support of the team as we looked to progress through the tournament.

Our transport to the ground was by two hire cars with Murray driving one of them. Whether he was nervous of driving abroad or something, I don't know but one of his famed road rage moments occurred when a French women upset him on the road. She stepped off the kerb into the path of the car and Murray had to slam the brakes on. Leaning out of the window he shouted, "Ouvree les ouefs! Bloody stupid woman!" What he'd meant when he shouted to her in anger was, 'open your eyes,' which explained the smile and laugh she gave him which made the situation worse for Murray as he continued to barrate her about laughing. It made it all the more hilarious for the rest of us as we shouted at the women, "Open your eggs, can't you see us with those eggs!" Oh dear, another legendary moment and another French phrase to remember for life, with a smile.

The ground in Toulouse was very much like a traditional English football ground and we were there in good time to gain access, this time without any hitches from the security staff. We found ourselves behind the goal on the lower tier of a two tiered stand which isn't ideal for us but never mind we were in and ready. Murray banged the drum and the roar went up from the England fans, it always appears louder to us when we're under a roof but we know that the upper tier can't hear us as well as if it was behind them. Still the sound was good and the game started well enough with both sides cancelling each other out, 0-0 at half time. Youngsters, Beckham and Owen, were running the show but early in the second half Romania scored. That wasn't in the script but it was the signal for us to respond and try to encourage more vocal support by blowing and banging a bit harder. The fans responded and in the 83rd minute Michael Owen scored to level things up. The crowd went wild and urged the lads on to get another.

Disaster! In the last minute of normal time Dan Petrescu one of our former Sheffield Wednesday heroes took advantage of poor defending by England and scored a goal that was almost impossible to come back from. Try as we might in the four minutes added time we couldn't score, despite Michael Owen doing his best and hitting the post. It wasn't to be and we lost 2-1 but all was not lost if we at least got a draw against Columbia we'd be through to the knock out stages.

We were knackered that night, what with the heat and travelling, so slept well before having to get up early to go back home to work for two days and then get the plane back out for the Columbia game in Lens which was so close that it was almost in England. We joked at the time that it was like playing Arsenal with the French connection because it was so close to England. We travelled home via Charles De Gaulle airport in Paris after leaving Nice and were to change there and fly on to Luton.

On arrival at Charles De Gaulle we had limited time to catch the next flight and often there is an airport representative to meet you when things are close time wise just to direct you in the right way. No such thing happened on this occasion so not exactly being novices we headed for the check-in desk for Luton. All was well and we were directed to gate 36 to board but told to hurry as it was getting late. All running as best we could the first few of us got to the gate and we waited for Bram, Brian and Julie who were bringing up the rear. Once they'd caught up we had our boarding cards checked and went down the corridor towards the plane. At the end of the corridor was a staircase so we went down the stairs to the glass doors at the bottom turned left through the double doors and made the short walk to the plane steps. Up the steps and into the plane to find a French cleaner with the vacuum going cleaning the front seats. Rather stupidly we asked her if this was the plane for Luton and realising that she'd no idea what we were talking about we didn't wait for an answer as all ten of us ran back down the plane steps assuming that the next plane on the runway would be ours.

So, like something from the Keystone Cops or Benny Hill, we ran across the runway to the next plane, up the steps and in only to find that this time there was a pilot and his crew sat in the front seats of the plane eating their packed lunches. I don't know who was most shocked, so, we turned around, back down the steps and across the runway again, ten of us with instruments and bags, back in the building, up the stairs and back up the corridor, that is usually only one way, to emerge back in the terminal building much to the surprise of the girl who had checked us out about ten minutes prior.

She then explained that when we went down the staircase to the plane we should have turned right and boarded a bus that would have taken us to the correct plane. So off we went again down the corridor, stairs and onto the bus and the right plane. What a carry on, just a good job we weren't terrorists!

We arrived home and everyone was back on good terms with their work and home life when, after two days, we were back on our travels again for the all important Columbia game. Demand for tickets was even higher than normal, due to the close proximity, with notably more fans asking if anyone had tickets to sell. The ground was another one that resembled an English ground and this time we were again behind the goal but in a single-tiered stand that suited us fine.

This was a 'must win game' as far as we were concerned, going for the draw was too risky and all the media hype suggested that victory was everything as did England manager Glenn Hoddle. Even Prince William made it to the game which added to the singing of the national anthem somehow before the game. He did well though, with his helicopter landing right next to the stadium, enjoying only a short walk to the ground. We wondered if he joined in with the chanting having never got the chance to see from where we were sat.

You could feel the tension as the teams came out but there was an air of expectancy and the players looked confident. Off we went with the noise and the place was bouncing. We introduced Paul Ince's song which was two loud bangs on the drum followed by five quick bangs and

"Ince!" He liked it and so did the crowd, anything to give the lads a boost.

They had Valderrama in their team, who is remembered for his massive orange hair and for not being a bad player either but apart from him there were no household names to worry about, so we were confident.

The confidence was justified as Anderton put us in front in the twentieth minute and the volume was turned up a notch. It was as if those who had their worries had thrown them away and we were all singing together. A little later we got a free kick at our end right in front of us. Up stepped Beckham and from twenty five yards curled a screamer into the top corner. It was one of those that you could tell was going in from when he hit it and we were right in line. What a goal, it was party time, we were on our way to the next round. The Columbians needed to score three and they weren't good enough to score one really.

"We're not going home," to the tune off, 'Knees up mother Brown,' rang around the stadium from the England fans and how right we were as the final whistle went. England finished second in the group behind Romania and as the results filtered through we realised that this meant that we would be playing our arch enemy, Argentina, in the next round.

Chapter Ten

We arrived in St.Etienne quite late at night and found it to be quite a nice place. There was, however, a slight problem with the accommodation. An apartment had been booked for us in the old part of town but when we arrived there wasn't enough room for all of us to sleep comfortably. There was a double bed and a couple of pull outs for more than ten people so there was no way that we could fit in. The problem was that it was too late to worry now, there was no chance of getting anywhere else and we couldn't afford it anyway.

The apartment had a mezzanine floor with the double bed on it and strangely a very large bath indeed to the left. About four of us claimed the bed and thought bath time! With the others looking up wondering what was going on myself, Murray, Loz and Adolf thought no more of it, stripped naked and jumped in the bath. It wasn't that strange for us because we all played football together and I'd grown up with Loz so it wasn't unusual to us to have our bits out together but those downstairs weren't aware of all that especially Antonella and Julie who were duly shocked, the former screaming with laughter at us.

It wasn't a great night's sleep with all of us strewn over cushions wherever there was a bit of space and four in a double bed is quite a squeeze, not to mention the farting, better not to actually. The main reason for the lack of sleep was that we were on the eve of one of the most important England games for years. We needed to win the game to progress to the quarter final stages of the World Cup and if we did we would eliminate Argentina.

No England fan needs reminding that Argentina's Maradona cheated in the 1986 World Cup when he handled the ball to score a goal against us that stood also due to poor refereeing. Maradona claimed after the game that it was the hand of God that scored the goal. What a load of absolute garbage, he cheated and should have admitted he did. To claim that it was the hand of God made it worse. He was a cheat and happy to make up a story to try and justify it! We needed to avenge that wrong doing, justice needed to prevail. If you add the whole aspect of the Falklands war a few years earlier and some say you shouldn't think about that because it's football, well, regardless this was a match with more than an edge to it.

Again we were determined to get to the ground early as positioning at the back of the stadium is imperative to us. When we arrived there was already a lot of activity going on around the stadium and TV crews were following fans about. A particularly large group coming down the road towards us to the sound of an Argentinean drum were attracting a lot of attention. Not being ones to miss an opportunity and certainly with an in-built desire to show that England's support was louder and better than theirs we struck up the band and proceeded to blow them away. We were far louder than them, we knew we would be, they were musicians, not fans, so it's always going to be us that wins, we're trained differently. Their dancers were better than ours, long legged with feathers from memory, now there's an idea for the future. What we had done though was establish the fact that we were louder than them so we'd won an important battle before we'd kick off. If they were what was to generate Argentinean support we'd beaten them already.

It was the same story as usual inside the stadium. We were behind the goal with the Argentines behind the other goal but the two sides of the ground were full of England fans including, Ulrika Jonson, and, in our end, in the stand to our right, was Mick Jagger. Let me tell you the sight of Mick Jagger singing along to us playing 'The Great Escape' is some strange feeling, but why not? I've sung many of his songs before. There were even England fans in the Argentina end but there wasn't a hint of crowd trouble.

As the teams came out they might as well have been at Wembley such was the roar from the crowd. There was a tension in the air, this was the best side that we'd played so far and then there was the history.

The band struck up straight away and the support was fantastic. I don't know where he came from but some guy in shorts and a bandana came to stand in front of us to scream and shout his head off and encourage us to do more and more which we welcomed. It was absolutely red hot that day especially at the back of the stand but once you're wet with sweat you're wet and when you're giving your all towards supporting England you don't care anyway.

What a game! Argentina scored after six minutes through Batistuta which signalled a rallying call from the fans and team with the response coming from Shearer four minutes later. Then on sixteen minutes the wonder kid Michael Owen set off on a darting run that ended with one of the best England goals ever scored and one that we'll remember forever. From the right side of the box he banged it into the top left hand corner, get in! We went berserk, absolutely mad. The guy in the bandana became our new best friend, we come back from one down and were flying.

All of us were playing as loud as possible, fans singing as loud as possible, non-stop and dripping with sweat, team and fans were sticking it up the Argies and it felt great. At last revenge.

We had a number of chances notably, Paul Ince from 35 yards, cue his new song. All looked well as we approached half time until Sol Campbell, a colossus of a man during the qualifiers, especially in Rome, fouled on the edge of our box. The Argentineans had obviously been practicing free kicks on the training ground because the resultant free kick was, it has to be said, an excellent set piece that we couldn't cope with and they scored to make it 2-2 at half time.

Time for a breather and to take some water on board. Murray could ring his shirt out and the brass players got valuable rest for their lips, as brass players will know your lips just pack in and go numb after so long due to restricted blood flow. That couldn't happen today.

The teams emerged for the second half with no changes, the very tall Danish referee Nielson carrying the ball to the centre spot for the kick off. Barely a minute of the second half had passed when Beckham was fouled by Simeone and as Beckham lay on the floor he kicked out at him with his leg. It was nothing other than petulance probably fired by the situation but the reaction of Simeone was as big an overreaction as you will see any where. It had the desired affect and Beckham was sent off. As far as we were concerned it was the Argentineans cheating again, a matter of interpretation but that's how we saw it.

This had the effect of spurring us, the crowd and the team on even more than before, if it were possible. We'd played them off the park but they'd managed to score twice and now by cheating they'd managed to reduce us to ten men.

We blew, banged, shouted, clapped for the remaining forty four minutes of the half cheering the ten men on as if our life depended on it. The Argentineans had a penalty appeal turned down when they thought Adams had handled, we then went straight down the other end and from a perfect cross Campbell headed the ball into the Argentinean net. Goooooaaaaaaaaaaaaaaallll!!!!!!!!!!!!!!! Oh yes! The ground erupted again as the players celebrated and there were only nine minutes left but wait a minute the referee had disallowed it.

Disallowing it is bad enough but he'd let them restart the game when the majority of our players were still celebrating the goal and they were on the attack, their entire team against three of our men and David Seaman. Once we'd realised the crowd yelled to the players who were celebrating to get back and the panic was there to see. Thankfully Darren Anderton had stayed alert and managed to intercept the attack and buy enough time for our players to regroup.

Within seconds I and the rest of the England support had gone from sheer ecstasy to a feeling of utter horror as we thought that we'd won the game to a situation where again very unfairly Argentina may have won the match. Football can be a very cruel game indeed.

At the end of ninety minutes it finished 2-2. The ten men of England were knackered and so were we, what a game. Extra time came and apart from a couple of chances it was an endurance test for the players and, once again, we played non-stop throughout encouraged by bandana man. We were more than grateful for the supply of water from the England fans that seemed to go in at the mouth and come straight out of the rest of our bodies such was the heat and effort being put in.

The team had played for 120 minutes, 75 of the minutes with only ten men, it was a fantastic performance and now it would be decided on penalties. Penalties! We'd gone out of Italia 90 on penalties and

Euro 96 we all knew that our record in penalty shoot outs wasn't the best but records are there for breaking. It's well written that things didn't go our way, they missed one penalty and we missed two, the end, we lost.

There was no justice, in fact it had made things worse, surely we deserved to win that game. Ten men for an hour and fifteen minutes and having gone out twice previously to penalties in previous competitions, surely we deserved to win. Unfortunately it doesn't work like that. We just sat there totally drained, still dripping wet along with a fair number of England fans reflecting on what should have been, some in tears. We'd all given our best on and off the field and it wasn't to be, it wasn't fair, we would get that revenge one day if there was any justice.

That was the end of the road for France '98 for England and us. We were absolutely distraught, it's not something you can help if you're as emotionally involved as we are. When your team loses it affects you. The thing that helped us get over this one was that the team gave their absolute all and did us proud.

Rupert and the Cutting Edge film crew had just about finished their filming now having a lot of the footage they needed for their programme. We'd arranged to meet them in a restaurant afterwards to say goodbye really but we heard that smelly footed Charlie was coming who deserved a parting shot from us.

Sat at a round table for ten the plan was hatched. We arrived first and Rupert and Charlie were to join us. They should have realised when they sat down that we were unusually protected by our napkins with most of our bodies covered. The reason being that the attack signal was as soon as Charlie sat down in front of his tomato soup bowl. He did so and from every angle came bits of bread rolls and croutons directed into his soup that splashed rather pleasingly all over him repeatedly like a machine gun scene from The Godfather. Cruel? No, he deserved it, I hope he's sorted his feet out now.

Early group Photo - Wembley '97

Russ Williams Virgin Radio '97

The tour bus that never was

Helen Chamberlain in action with the band at Wembley

Richard Branson's V2 Staff in SWFC shirts London '98

MOROCCO '98 with World Cup Willy

Celebrating 2-2 draw

Street Football in Morocco

End of the game in Morocco

The Band with Melinda Messenger

Melinda in our Village Sunday Team shirt

With Brazilian Samba Band

The Band on Richard and Judy Show

Radio 1 FRANCE '98

Radio 1 Lightning Seeds

Ready for action - first game France '98

Loz

Emperor Bram

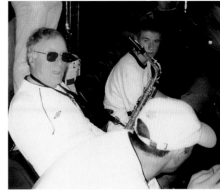

Negotiating with the French Police about Drumsticks!

Loz (with hair),
Melinda Messenger
and Murray
France '98

Murray and I
enjoyed it
anyway!

In bed with World Cup Willy

Murray, Chris (World Cup Willy) and I
during the National Anthem

Marseilles, France '98

Switzerland

Private jet to France anyone?

Rugby League Final Debut

Ian Wright with the Band after his TV Show
in our Sunday Team shirt

Take That's Mark Owen V2000 5-a-side

"The Man" Stuart Hall

The Limo - Sheffield Station

Chapter Eleven

We left France behind, as another tournament that promised so much but alas didn't deliver the World Cup victory that we and the country believe we should have every time we're in a major tournament. The record flopped too, although at least it made the charts which we were pleased about, any thoughts of being mega rich pop stars with a Three Lions type hit were long gone, not that they were there in the first place. We'd had a great time and the documentary was due to be shown on Channel 4 soon but it is the football that matters to us and we'd been knocked out so we finished the tournament proud but downbeat (excuse the pun) because we should have still been there.

A full account of our exploits was given in a diary report each day in the local Sheffield paper, I suppose it was an early form of twitter which a lot of fans back home followed. We'd had our fair share of press and met people that we wouldn't have otherwise. The Sun had done us proud too helping us with the travel so we weren't downhearted there's always the next game to put things right. Even the 'Cutting Edge' documentary went out to good reviews and showed us in a good light. The only 'edge' that was there was a fall out about taxi's and the rest showed the passion and level of support that we give to what we do which was pleasing knowing how films can be edited to show whatever the producer wants but we trusted Rupert from the start and he didn't let us down.

Such is international football that the draw had already taken place for the European Championships and England had drawn Sweden, Bulgaria, Luxembourg and Poland. We always seemed to draw Poland no matter what tournament it was and Euro 2000 was going to be no different.

There was a bit of a deflated period after France '98 but we soon got around to September and our first Euro 2000 fixture which was away in Sweden. Our flight to Sweden was from Stansted which you should be able to do easily in an hour and a half from Sheffield. All the guys will tell you that my timekeeping can leave us a little close to the mark sometimes but this particular trip took the biscuit. We arrived in three cars at Stansted in good time as far as we could see and parked up in the airport car park and caught the bus to the terminal. When we got into the terminal we found the flight on the departures board as usual and went to the desk to check in to be told that we'd missed it. "What do you mean missed it?"

"It leaves in forty minutes and the flight is closed", said one of those check-in ladies with a tone of finality. Now that's not what you want to hear having travelled the length of the country to catch the plane in the first place but we'd got a sponsor for the trip too and they wouldn't be best pleased if they'd paid and we missed the flight, not to mention that we wouldn't have been too chuffed ourselves.

Two West Ham fans in front of us said, "Oh well, that's that then," and went home but we'd come further than them and it was inconceivable that we weren't going. Quick thinking prevailed and I said to the staff, "It can't be closed, it's usually only twenty minutes before it leaves that the desk closes, isn't it?"
"Not anymore", with a stern voice.
"But we didn't know it'd changed".
"It's in the booking conditions".
"Isn't there anything we can do because we're the band that are playing the national anthems on the pitch at the England game in Sweden and obviously we need to be there or there won't be any".

A chink of light appeared as she said that the only way she could let us on now was is if the pilot agrees. A moments prayer and a phone call to the pilot resulted in the check-in lady coming back to us and saying that the pilot had agreed to let us on. Whoever the pilot was that day we'd like to say, thank you. He must have been an England fan and our luck was in. That led to the usual banter from the rest of the band about being late and me telling them they worry too much, I'll always sort it out.

The requirement has happened on too many occasions but it's always been alright in the end.

With a massive sigh-of-relief we boarded the plane, waving to the pilot on the way up the steps to say thank you and believe me we were more than grateful. We vowed never to let it happen again knowing full well that it probably would.

We landed in Sweden for the game that was in Stockholm even though, as sometimes happens, we end up coming through an obscure airport nowhere near the city. Rumours go around the support that it's because the police can manage the supporters better but more likely is that it was cheaper for the tour operator than landing at a major airport. Whatever the reason it does happen and, hey hum, at least we're there which is the main thing. We got the usual welcoming party of security staff and police with Loz managing not to trip over anything on the way in as he did in Morocco, so, we arrived at the car rental desk unhindered.

A mini bus had been pre-booked and for some reason Jimmy was allocated as the driver which was a first for us. There seemed to be a shortage of transport into the city because this was clearly a small airport and one of the people struggling to get a lift was Clive Allen the former England, Tottenham. Arsenal and Palace striker. "Any chance of a lift?" For Clive Allen, of course there was chance. We all piled into the bus, instruments and all, with Clive in the second row back. He was sort of familiar - he'd starred in our video for the World Cup single even though we didn't meet him then.

Murray and I shared the double front passenger seat and began to regret it after only a few minutes. Jimmy had never driven a mini bus before and couldn't get to grips with the width of the vehicle never mind the left hand drive. Put the two together and it was a recipe for disaster. With the nerves jangling and having had to shout warnings, on more than one occasion, we approached the outskirts of Stockholm with a view to dropping Clive off first and then finding our own hotel.

Remarkably we came across Clive's hotel which was naturally quite a large quality establishment in the city centre across the dual-carriageway from us, behind the bus station. Clive pointed it out and then the madness of Jimmy's driving took over. Whatever he was thinking I don't know but he decided to get to the hotel, more or less as the crow flies, which meant going the wrong way through the one way bus station with buses coming at us from all angles. The screaming reached a crescendo when we just missed a bus, careered across the dual-carriageway, mounted the central reservation and came off it with a bump on the other side, straight across the other dual-carriageway and into the hotel forecourt where the guy's face at the front of house was an absolute picture. Never mind him, Clive Allen shot out of the bus as quickly as he could, grabbing his bag and saying thanks as he left with obvious feelings of disbelief at Jimmy's driving and the fact that he'd made it in one piece. On we went to our hotel, dropped off our stuff, usual fight for beds and out into Stockholm.

Driving around the city we came across a bar that looked quite lively and it's always going to be pot luck where you go so the decision was taken to go in. All seemed fine once we'd sussed out that there weren't any 'bad lads' in there so little danger of any trouble. We're quite a friendly bunch and like to interact with the locals so anyone that wants to chat is welcomed into the group and either them, us or both usually, end up having a good laugh into the bargain. On this occasion a really big Swedish bloke decided to join us so we started chatting away to him and then I noticed that the guys had started to move away leaving just a few of us and the guy mainly concentrating on me. The guy was a bit strange and aggressive in some ways with his opinions and was becoming a bit too friendly. The other lads had moved away as it was clear to them that this bloke fancied me. Now I'm all for live and let live but I'm not up for trying everything and certainly I'm not in any way shape or form anywhere near being homosexual, not ever, ever. The problem being this guy was about six feet eight and built like a brick shithouse, aggressive and after me.

A quiet word with Jimmy to get the minibus, tell everyone else and when you pull up outside sound the horn and get ready. The guys left the bar in ones and twos and the minibus arrived outside which was my signal to run and run I did. Out of the door at the top of the bar as fast as I could, down the footpath and diving into the minibus Jimmy took off, much to the amusement of everyone else but I was safe at least. "Bugger me! No, forget that! What was that all about?"

Still hungry we found our way to a Chinese restaurant far enough away for me to relax again. Why did we pick this particular restaurant? Simply because it was called the 'Minge Garden.' Much in the same way that we picked the 'Fooking Restaurant' when we were in China Town in London - it's a bloke thing. Great food and a new song was born based on the old song, 'I beg your pardon? I never promised you a Minge Garden.' We serenaded the clientele in the restaurant with the majority joining in, after a few funny looks the waiters were alright with it too.

The game was the next day and it was important, the first of our European qualifier campaign that should lead to us competing in Euro 2000 in Holland and Belgium. Sweden is a very nice place and the people are too so we felt at ease spending our time in the lead-up to the game people watching, we wanted to make sure that it was true what they say about Swedish girls being tall, blonde and beautiful and we can confirm that it is true! Arriving at the ground, early as usual, there was a relaxed atmosphere and we entered the ground, which was modern with quite high stands but close to the pitch, which was good.

Unusually there was no Beckham in the line up that day as he was serving his two-match suspension from the World Cup which some fans were pleased about, blaming him for the loss to Argentina when he got sent off. Some idiots had even hung an effigy of him from a pub in London, very short memories some people. Determined as ever we started up on kick off and didn't have to wait long until we were celebrating a Shearer goal. That was more like it, we're on our way again, victory in our sights. "Great Escape," I'd shout down the line and Max would do his snare drum introduction, now familiar to

England fans, who were in fine voice. We dominated the game and ten minutes later England's wonder kid, Michael Owen, scored only to have it ruled out for offside. That was the signal to turn up the volume, if that were possible, we were beginning to enjoy ourselves.

With our experience we should have known that things would turn against us and after half an hour they did, Sweden scored twice in two minutes and try as we might for the remainder of the game the score line remained the same at the final whistle. When things aren't going England's way some fans get restless and pick on whoever is around them at the time, some even have a go at us but we're not ones to shy away from any banter, or bullying for that matter, and any attempts to have a go are met with fierce resistance from us. Having heard most comments before we have the well rehearsed answers in our armoury that results in the attacker either being laughed at or coming round to our way of thinking rather quickly.

It was different after that game though, the disappointment boiled over into anger and there was trouble after the game from a few idiots who hurled beer barrels through a floor to ceiling window at the back of the stand, down onto the crowd below. I didn't see anyone injured, luckily, but I did see some arrests including one fan that we knew who ended up getting banned for life. Was it worth it?

Yes, we were disappointed as Jimmy drove us back to the airport where we had a hotel booked before the early morning flight the next day. Clive Allen hadn't given us a call for a lift back. We arrived at the airport and had instructions for the hotel nearby but could we find it? Could we hell. We went all over the place in the forest and countryside, nobody about to ask, even at the airport because it was one of these obscure ones. After hours of searching the decision was taken to sleep in the mini bus at the airport, the flight was at 7.00 a.m. anyway so we'd have to be at the airport for 5.30 a.m. at the latest. There were some England fans at the airport already and every available place that looked remotely comfortable inside the airport was taken so we'd be better in the minibus. We parked up, the only vehicle in the three hundred spaced car park and attempted to sleep. It was freezing, only September but Swedish September and even though the heater was on in the bus it was difficult to get warm never mind comfortable. There's always someone farting or coughing or just talking, the farts in particular would keep anyone awake and I mean the smell, not the noise. I even had a spell lying on a piece of polystyrene in the luggage compartment but that was the coldest spot of the lot.

It was shortly after that that we heard a knock on the steamed up side door window. It was about 3.00 a.m., who could this be?

"It's the coppers."

"You're joking, the farts weren't that bad!"

Opening the door I said, "Good evening."

"You have parked in the police parking bay and must move immediately."

There were now two vehicles in the three hundred spaced car park, us and him and we'd got his spot, could you believe it on two counts, one the rotten luck and two that he couldn't park in another bay just for this time. Apparently some policemen are like that, even in Sweden.

The bus was moved and we settled down again to hear another knock on the door. Stood there were two West Ham fans who asked if we would mind if they could sit in our minibus because they were freezing outside. Obligingly we let them in but twenty minutes later they were forced out by the pungency of the farts, leaving us their thanks but they couldn't stand it anymore.

It was just too cold, something had to be done, so stepping out of the bus we realised that the car park had a small island in the middle with zebra crossings on each side, flashing lights and a bit of a chicane going on on one side. That was it! A trolley grand prix that would keep us warm, everyone was to get a luggage trolley turn it round and use it in a scooter like fashion to propel themselves around the track as quickly as possible, first one home was the winner. Word went round the airport and other, equally freezing fans, joined the starting grid making a field of about thirty would-be Swedish grand prix winners revving their engines, raring to go. The lights went to green and off they went. Absolute chaos ensued. The trolleys have a life and direction of their own under normal conditions but throw in an element of competition and they were going in all directions. Spectacular crashes resulted with three going over the handlebars when they gripped the brake bar by mistake in the excitement, it was more like the Grand National than a grand prix. Most spectacular was Jimmy, who when in the lead, with only a few yards to go, managed to go over his handlebars and lose the race at the last minute. No trolleys were damaged in the making of the race but lots of bodies suffered although it did, as predicted, warm us all up.

Dawn came with the news that one of the two planes back to England was delayed. Yes, you're right, it was our plane that was delayed for at least four hours so back into the minibus in the search for breakfast. We took a right turn out of the airport and then first right and to our disbelief arrived at the very hotel that we should have been staying in the previous night, the one that we spent hours looking for.

The plane was delayed a lot longer than the four hours that we were told which led to additional problems with work for most of the lads (and lass) having not booked the day off. This in turn leads to other halves having a go at us in some cases because it means a day's holiday lost for them. We did eventually arrive home and the blagging and excuses flowed for us all.

Chapter Twelve

The mood wasn't good in the country having lost to Sweden but there was a chance to put it right in the double header at home to Bulgaria and away to Luxembourg in October.

Our enthusiasm never, ever, wanes and we had a special guest to perk us up for the Bulgaria game in Soccer AM's Helen Chamberlain. We'd met Helen when we'd been on Soccer AM which seemed to be every week at one time and we got on really well. Another proper football fan Helen fitted in well with her snare drum last seen at Torquay and she'd had the banter like the rest of us, right up our street. We got on so well that Helen even persuaded us to make a couple of guest appearances in support of Torquay when there were no Sheffield Wednesday games. This was when Wednesday were Premier League and Torquay bottom end of the Fourth division so it didn't matter surely, Wednesday wouldn't ever fall that far (nearly did of course). So it was that we turned up at Boothferry Park, Hull's old ground for a midweek Torquay away game. There were more of us in the band than Torquay fans or it was very close at least but we managed to inspire victories on both occasions. It was from Helen that we learned the ''Ince'' chant as she sang it for Torquay's goalie Reece. The best airing of that chant though was when used for Andy Booth at Hillsborough, Andy's surname lending itself to being able to chant with some real gusto.

The meeting place was at the top of Wembley Way for the game and when everyone had arrived, including Max, on time this time, we entered the stadium. We had to be inside the stadium three hours before kick off but the FA did give us a packed lunch and look after us very well. Trevor was on the door and Barbara, a large West Indian lady with an infectious laugh and sense of humour, whilst at the same time having the knack of being able to control us with just a look. Our position in the old Wembley Stadium was behind the school kids section so we had plenty of enthusiastic voices from the off. The position was mid way between the old tunnel and the dug out so ideal for playing a particular tune for Alan Smith, the England physio, as he walked past us to his seat. Alan would always give us a wave when we played his song which was great, a comforting feeling, sort of homely.

The match didn't live up to expectations and despite one or two good chances we didn't manage to get the all important goal that would have satisfied the nation with a win. On such occasions the crowd turns and boos were heard at the end of the game. Although we would never boo England one can understand the fans giving their verdict after the final whistle, but only after the final whistle, until then the game can be won when it's 0-0. We shared the disappointment but were looking forward to the Luxembourg game which should be a certain victory.

For the first time we'd decided to drive to an England away game. I'd had a look on the map and it wasn't that far to Luxembourg, about the same as northern Scotland, there was the channel to cross of course but we'd got a tunnel now, so easy. We hired a VW minibus from local company, Gilders, and nine of us set off to Folkstone to catch the train, three days after the disappointment of Wembley. We set off in the early hours of Wednesday morning, the day of the game, ready to get to the channel tunnel for about 7.00 a.m. After a short delay boarding we found ourselves in France by 8.00 a.m. trying to find the road to Belgium. It was my turn to drive and even though I say it myself there was nothing to it, I'd driven abroad quite a bit so, on we went. We stopped in a cafe and had lunch before the Belgium boarder and crossed over into Belgium without a problem.

The road conditions were good and even when it started to rain it wasn't too bad until the traffic started to build up in front of us. We weren't familiar with the roads and didn't really know how long we had to go until we got to the Luxembourg border. The traffic cleared after about an hour and we carried on, a bit of moaning about being too late for the game but just good banter. Then the heavens opened and it really did start to pore it down which began to worry us, traffic was at a standstill now which was no good to us. It went dark quite early as the game was in mid October which didn't help the traffic or our sense of direction and the doubts as to whether or not we would make the game were aired more frequently, to which I would reply, "Don't worry, it'll be alright."

The rain became more intense, if that were possible, as we arrived at the Luxembourg border which looked familiar from a European Sheffield Wednesday trip (yes, we have had a European tour). A bit of a chat with the border police who ask the daftest questions like, "Are you going to the football match?" Nine of us in a minibus with England shirts on. No, of course not we just fancied a trip over. So, trying to conform we kept straight faces and made it through the border into Luxembourg. I knew we were home and dry time wise because the police hadn't said we'd never make it and if there'd been a chance we'd miss the game they'd have said it I'm sure. Fortunately, Luxembourg isn't that big, so we managed to find the ground without any trouble. We parked up near the stadium at 7 p.m. for a 7.30 p.m. kick off. "There you go, told you it'd be alright," I said, to a barrage of abuse coming from the back of the bus.

We got absolutely soaked to the skin on the way to the ground that was only about 500 yards away. When we got to the stadium the turnstiles were too small for the instruments to get through so we had to arrange to go through a different gate. It was then that we realised we'd lost a ticket but fortunately, maybe due to the rain or the confusion of us arriving on mass and needing to get through the different gate, it wasn't noticed. It wasn't that we hadn't paid so nothing was lost really. When we got into the ground it was standing on the terrace anyway and because it was raining it was an open terrace, naturally.

The game itself delivered what was expected really. There were only 8,000 fans there, which made the stadium full, about 7,850 England fans and the rest home fans, it must wear them down losing every game. It was a sort of anti climax game, we gave it our all but because we were in the open air and because England were expected to win the atmosphere was a bit flat. In fairness when its throwing it down with rain in the open it doesn't help the singing or playing especially with water running down your neck. England scored through wonder kid, Owen, again and Shearer added to the score on forty minutes. The second half was a bit more frustrating though and we didn't make it 3-0 until the ninetieth minute through Gareth Southgate, for his first international goal. It should have been more but the England fans, including us, were happy to have won and have three points following the recent performances. At least we were still able to qualify for Euro 2000.

Once the game had finished it was back to the minibus via a line of leather clad police. We played a few songs on the way back and the stern-looking police changed their mood which was probably based on what they'd been briefed rather than what they'd witnessed. The two situations were miles apart and I can remember England fans even dancing with the police, willingly joining in as we went past. Just how it should be, singing in the rain.

Adolf drove us back to the channel tunnel in true German fashion. It seemed a breeze now that we were experienced European drivers but we were all looking and feeling a bit tired so some had drifted off to sleep.

It's always a dangerous thing to fall asleep in our company, various things can happen to you. For example any of your food will be eaten or interfered with so that you get a surprise when you wake up. Various things will be placed up your nose, in your ears or mouth. The favourite trick, often used on planes, is to just drip a considerable amount of water into the lap of whoever is asleep and then summon the stewardess to point out that we think they've had a little accident.

On reaching good old blighty again it was Murray's turn to drive. We'd all been awake now for over 24 hours but we had deadlines to be back for so had to keep going. Some took the risk and slept. Bram was OK because nobody would do anything to him out of respect but Murray, now realising he should have had a kip at some stage during the journey, was really struggling which meant I didn't want to nod off in case he did and make it the last trip we made anywhere. If we had match sticks Murray would have used them, however, all we could do was stop at almost every service station on the way home. It slowed us down but at least we arrived home in one piece and immediately went to the toilet, shower and bed in that order. Great fun driving over and through Europe but next time I think we'll have a stop over and maybe arrive more than half an hour before kick off.

There were a couple of friendly games at Wembley against Czechoslovakia and World Cup winners, France, before the next competitive game, Euro 2000 qualifying match. We beat the Czechs and lost to France which didn't set the fans on fire but losing to the World champions I suppose could be excused, although I still can't view France as that strong a footballing nation. The real talking points though before the France game surrounded the manager's job, Glenn Hoddle, who allegedly made some comments about disabled people, karma and former lives which caused quite a stir amongst the press and the country as a whole. As a result Glenn Hoddle was sacked as England manager and Howard Wilkinson took charge of the national team for the defeat against France.

Speculation was rife about who would succeed Glenn Hoddle as manager with every name under the sun being put forward as usual. We were sad to see Glenn go because it was him that gave us the chance to do our stuff for England in 1996 and we weren't sure if the new manager would want us to continue.

Despite the anxiety, some more anxious than others in the band, we needn't have worried as the new manager was Kevin Keegan, the people's champion, a good Yorkshireman and a reputation for playing attractive attacking football and of bonding with the fans wherever he'd managed teams before. Kevin wears his heart on his sleeve which most fans like and has an evident passion. That's not always the case with other managers and fans like that too. It was the start of a new era, we were up for it and so was he. The first game was to be the Euorpean Championship qualifying game against our old favourites, Poland, at Wembley, now that sounded familiar.

Chapter Thirteen

England football had been invigorated by the appointment of Kevin Keegan as manager. Kevin was a popular appointment although it was very unusual, if not a first, that the previous manager had been sacked for non-football reasons.

So it was that the first game of the Keegan era arrived and we set off for Wembley in the limo that we were hiring for the trips at the same price as a mini bus including the driver we all had our places usually me, Murray and Adolf on the back seat and at the other end would be Jimmy, Denton and Max and in between Bram, Brian and Julie, who would get caught in the cross fire of apples, plastic pellets from toy guns, elastic bands, water and anything else that could be hurled down the car, often in the dark when the light switch was thrown. There was actually one occasion when the driver had to stop due to the activity in the back that was making him swerve a little too much. We put it down to over excitement; we hyped ourselves up so much for the games that it wasn't surprising that some of that energy bubbled over.

There was quite a presence in the team of Manchester United players with the well-publicised youth from the early nineties coming through and with the Neville brothers, Gary and Phil, David Beckham and Paul Scholes now very well established on the side and Andy Cole (as he was then not Andrew). The games were greatly influenced by the Manchester United quintet but Paul Scholes took the man of the match award for his hat trick of fine goals scoring twice before Poland replied and hitting his third in the second half to finish the game off.

The crowd were inspired by the team's performance and Keegan's appointment but most of all because we'd got three valuable points towards qualifying for Euro 2000. The Great Escape rang out well around Wembley that night and we gave it our all. We even got a letter from a school in Bristol who wrote to the FA to say that their experience had been enhanced and made so much better by having seats near to us, and we very much appreciated this. I always carry ear plugs for the poor unfortunate people who don't like us and can't bring themselves to join in and spur the team. To this end we always do a quick scan of the crowd immediately in front of us to offer those who we consider look like they may need ear plugs the benefit of our goodwill. This usually breaks the ice with people and they end up singing along with everyone. The atmosphere was getting louder and more positive at Wembley which we were pleased about. Kevin Keegan praised the fans after his first Wembley game and it pleased us that the team off the pitch got some recognition.

England away games were still very different from home games with a fair share of idiots travelling to certain ones. The Hungary friendly match wasn't one of these games, and faces that were once new became friends, whether that be a knowing nod or a bit of banter signalling an acceptance that we were welcomed. In Budapest we found ourselves in the British Bulldog pub and met a guy called Andy Liney for the first time. Andy was clearly a character and the banter started from the off. We found out that Andy was a Doncaster Rovers fan, in fact he was the fans' director on the board and also the Donny Dog which was the Doncaster mascot. A great lad and we were to see Andy on just about every England trip for years to come. He would tell us some wonderful stories, one about his three strikes and out public warning letters from the Football League for his mascot antics. The first, in costume of course, was for cocking his leg up and pretending to wee up against the corner flag during a game, the second was when he took a red and white wig from a fan and during a break in a game placed it on the opposition goalie's bald head and, last but not least, he once got a little too amorous with one of those furry microphones that TV companies place around the pitch, shall we say, 'doggy style'.

In Hungary we learnt about the Danube separating Buda and Pest and that there were some decent bargains in the market but there wasn't much football to talk of, the game ending 1-1 in a typically friendly fashion. We were on a day trip which had become our preferred way of travelling as they were cheaper and quicker than other options which helped with cost and the all important time off work. The down-side being that they are absolutely knackering as you are awake for thirty hours or more, often with a long drive from a southern airport when you land. Still, needs must.

The next meaningful England home game was against Euro 2000 group leaders, Sweden, and was one of those frustrating affairs when we needed to win but just couldn't score a goal. It was Alan Shearer's fiftieth appearance, surely he would celebrate that with a goal. No, he wouldn't and at the end of the game it left England needing to win their remaining three qualifying games to get to Holland and Belgium the following year. We couldn't contemplate not qualifying and would do anything we could to help qualification.

What we didn't expect to do was to be asked to go on TFi Friday, the fashionably trendy TV show on Channel 4, dressed as nuns. The show was hosted by Chris Evans and written in part by Danny Baker, who we respected as a football radio genius. I loved the show with all its quirky bits and it looked as if we were to become one of them. We all blagged off work and the other activities that we once again should have been doing and turned up at the studios by the river in West London. It was an experience entering the studio and sharing a green room with proper artists. There were rehearsals during the afternoon and then the show was recorded live which gave it the edge that made it a ratings winner. The band were to be playing in the bar. That was the best place to be on the show as you got to hear everything that was happening rather than in the main performing stage area which was a little detatched. Why we were dressed as nuns, no one ever told us, and we did witness the more professional, perfectionist side of Chris Evans when he arrived on set and insisted on a stage being built for us in the bar so that we could be seen. His words will still be ringing in the ears of those in charge of rehearsals and who didn't see that for themselves. That was the least of his worries that day, no one was aware but the show was to become quite legendary as the Happy Mondays lead singer, Shaun Rider, was on singing, 'Barcelona,' which was fantastic we being fans and all, but, the show went out at seven o'clock at night and the unscheduled, bad language from Shaun embarrassed Channel 4 such that future shows wouldn't be allowed to be broadcast live. One of those moments when we could say, we were there, I suppose.

More important things awaited, England had important games to win to guarantee qualification automatically to Euro 2000. Next stop Bulgaria on another exhausting day trip. When we landed in Bulgaria it was clear that it was quite a deprived place, most buildings were grey and not very well maintained by English standards. Our coach journey was bizarre. The commentary by the female guide lasted from the moment we got on the coach to when we got off, which seemed like a life time. All she spoke of was how bad Bulgaria was in every way possible and compared it to the greatness of England to the point of delivering the most unpolitically correct speech we've ever heard. Things like their royal family are ugly unlike our beautiful Princess Diana, to slagging off their economy and government, immigrants, the standard of living, how we won wars and bashed the Germans. It really was incredible and quite comical to listen to. Why she went off on one like that lord only knows, she said, "This is the business district; it's really not very good, it's all run down, not like your super city area in London," and on it went for an hour or more.

Sofia wasn't that bad and we had time to visit the market again where there was loads of lace prompting a doily style hat for each of us. Loz was able to purchase his customary doll for his cabinet at home whilst we looked at the antiques section that included Nazi and communist soldier's hat badges, etc., indicating a closeness to history that we don't have due to our geography.

The stadium for the game was a typically ex-communist block athletics arena with a running track around the pitch and open terraces that we didn't like because the noise disappears out of the stadium rather than transmitting towards the pitch. We scored early enough through Alan Shearer but they equalised almost straight away and blow and bang as much as we could there was no victory coming despite Bulgaria being reduced to ten men for the last quarter of an hour. The 1-1 result meant that England must win against Luxembourg and Poland later in the year to have a hope of qualifying. Qualification would then depend on other results in the group but there was a life-line, the chance of a play-off game if we were classed as one of the best runners up.

The game against Luxembourg proved to be the formality that it was always going to be with England triumphing 6-0 in front of an expectant crowd which left a trip to our old friends, Poland, where we needed to win to have a chance of qualifying or at least get a draw. After the Luxembourg game we played outside Wembley not realising the congestion that we would cause at the top of Wembley Way. It wasn't the best idea we'd had and although fun we didn't repeat the act at the request of the stewards and they were right too.

Another one of those awful open stadiums was the venue for this all important game in Warsaw. We had a deal with Admiral, the kit manufacturers, who supplied us with England clothing and leisure wear and they'd pushed the boat out reproducing the old Admiral England football shirts for this one. The shirts were the ones that Kevin Keegan used to wear as a player with the broad blue and red stripes across the top. Not only that, they'd provided us with Keegan wigs too, the long black permed version of the seventies, so we were ready. It was a sunny day and the wigs were extremely hot, especially when you're playing at full pelt or if you're a drummer. These kind of games bring out the extra mile from the support and there was a massive turn-out of England fans. We got our St.George flag up on the fence behind us along with all the rest and our usual position at the back of the crowd. The added bonus of being at the top of the terrace is that you can often see outside the stadium so that at England games you can begin to appreciate the crowd management we have at home and the value of getting into games early. When the crowd builds up prior to kick off inevitably it seems foreign grounds can't cope with the numbers and frustration gets the better of fans who begin to sense the beginning of the game and no prospect of seeing it. These are often flash points for trouble and Poland was no exception. Security was at its height which we'd learnt was the way in Poland and we soon found out why as the atmosphere turned aggressive on the terrace to our right amongst the Polish fans, just as before in Krakow rival Polish teams fight amongst themselves at international games.

That was up to them, we had an important game to win and set about playing as loud as possible, the national anthem, Rule Britannia, The Great Escape, England Till I Die, any and all the songs we could think of to get the team going. The Polish fans obviously didn't like what the band and the fans were doing as we out shouted the home support and the aggression started to be directed towards our terrace. To add to their frustration we were playing quite well. It was no surprise then when we were shot at with a flare from the terrace to our right. As we played I could see the flare coming right at us but we're English and things like that can't be allowed to put one off. With a shouted warning and a duck to the right, left in Murray's case, the act of audacity only served to produce extra vigour and determination that they were not going to beat us for volume that day. The flare hit our flag right behind us, so, we brushed it off and gained an extra reason to play that bit harder, they had nearly damaged our flag - now that wasn't on.

The game continued in the midst of all of this, England having various penalty claims turned down by the referee. We continued to play well but once again the goal that we so needed never materialised and the game ended 0-0. Not before David Battye had been sent off though for a second bookable offence, leaving us with ten men for the last seven minutes and to endure the inevitable period of time when we had our hearts in our mouth every time Poland came near our goal. If we'd have lost the game there's no way we'd have even come near to a play-off game but as it was we had a life-line, depending on the result of the Sweden v Poland game which would determine the best runner-up from our group and so if we were to progress to the one-off, play-off game, Sweden had to win.

We wouldn't know our fate until the day before the next friendly game against Belgium which was unusual as it was to be played away from Wembley, at Sunderland's Stadium of Light. A month after the Poland game we set off for Sunderland in the knowledge that Sweden had beaten Poland the day before and we had qualified for the play-offs. We also had a new gadget for this trip, a microphone that broadcast through the car's speakers. The possibilities were endless but we mainly used it for broadcasting to the general public various messages as we travelled up the A1 in several cars. The funniest moment came when we arrived at Sunderland and started to interview two girls live, masquerading as the local radio station. They were only convinced it was for real when they heard themselves coming out of the car radio in front, which was Loz's car, of course. However, when the questioning turned to questions that you wouldn't really expect on local radio they gave us a slap and continued on to the match.

We had a bit of experience of playing at the Stadium of Light with Sheffield Wednesday when the security staff insisted that we only played when the ball was out of play which was one of the biggest farces we'd ever been involved in but they came round that day in the end. That said we were a little apprehensive being away from Wembley for the first time and didn't know what to expect. We were right to be apprehensive. When we entered the stadium we were escorted to our position which was in a tunnel to the left of the goal at ground level. Clearly the sound wouldn't get out half as well as if we were in our usual spot of the back row of the stand so the atmosphere would suffer and it did. Despite trying to educate the ground staff it was too late because the stadium was full, so, rather than the positive stuff that we deliver, the negative, abusive and racist chants could be heard which is very disappointing when it could have been so different.

Although a friendly match, the game was quite exciting, with England scoring first. Belgium equalised and then a dodgy moment before Redknapp scored the winner, a twenty five yards effort for his first England goal. The goal was at our end and there was a mini pitch invasion as the players came to celebrate right in front of the tunnel that we were in. Just what we needed, a pitch invasion that engulfed us all on national television which would mean that when the analysis of the film would be done after the game who was in the middle of it all, us lot. I knew they shouldn't have put us there and it was all going horribly wrong. When we watched it back we could see certain heads of the band sticking up in the tunnel above those on the pitch but fortunately nothing came of it and we didn't have to defend ourselves or Sunderland's strange decision to put us there in the first place.

We have a fantastic relationship with the FA and particularly the englandfans staff which is the England supporters club. People like Ian Murphy, Nicola Jones, Richard Holloway and Jill Smith have looked after us very well throughout the years for which we are very grateful. After the Sunderland game we got together to try and make sure that we were never put in the wrong place again in any stadium, at least at a home game. This was going to be particularly important in the coming years because Wembley stadium was to be redeveloped and all England's home games would be played around the country at different venues and we would often only have one chance to get it right.

Saying goodbye to Sunderland we left happy with the result but disappointed with what had happened. It didn't, however, stop us broadcasting our various messages to different people on the way home from the car.

Then the news came through and any disappointment that we were feeling soon paled into insignificance as the draw for the play-off game was made. England would play two games, one home and one away to decide which team would go forward to Holland and Belgium in Euro 2000. Who did we draw? Why were we so ecstatic? We'd drawn SCOTLAND!!!!!!!!!!!!!!

Chapter Fourteen

I am one of the England fans that has been to an England v Scotland game at Wembley during the home internationals time and the 'friendly' matches afterwards. I went to the game after the famous Scottish pitch invasion when they broke the posts and was subject to untold abuse as I sat in the stand proudly in my England hat and scarf. How sweet it was to see Kevin Keegan and Trevor Brooking working together to score in that 3-1 victory. I was there again in 1981 when we lost due to a single goal by John Robertson for Scotland. The abuse that day was far worse than anything I experienced before as it was accompanied by being spat at continually throughout the match as we stood on the terrace at the old tunnel end of Wembley. We were at the back of the front terrace separated by a 30 foot drop before the area where the Scottish fans were in the tier above us. Consequently, nothing could be done to stop the spitting by anyone, police, stewards or otherwise, it was probably a good job that the 30 foot drop was between us for everyone's sake.

These things stick in one's mind and when we drew Scotland I thought this could be payback time, what goes around comes around and all that. Even though I have a few good Scottish friends and a Scottish godson and have enjoyed many great times visiting Scotland with the family in our caravan when I was younger. It was time they got beaten again by the English. They love us so much.......not, and we just love to beat them.

It's a strange feeling playing Scotland. You feel like you're following in your ancestor's footsteps, travelling north of the border into the modern equivalent of a full scale battle. One nation against another to claim bragging rights. If we didn't keep them in their place they would start crowing about Bannock Burn and their one victory over the English, when we battered them times many and are just chilled about it.

There wasn't much concentration on work in the week building up to the game. I'd hired a minibus for the trip that would start on Friday and we'd come back after the game on Saturday. I picked up the minibus on Friday, filled up with diesel and waited for the guys and Julie to arrive. We left from Wakefield, where I worked, so we could leave the cars safely and have enough time before we left to decorate the bus with about a hundred small plastic flags that we got from somewhere. We stuck them anywhere there was a hole, into the roof rack, wing mirrors, hinges, windows, absolutely anywhere and we had several bigger flags for the back and side windows. There was no mistaking that this was a bus of England fans travelling north for the game and with all the instruments in the back and on the roof too it would take Sherlock Holmes to figure out it was the band.

The plan was to go to Carlisle on the Friday, a sort of base camp before the English invasion the next day, again, much like our ancestors would have done in years gone by. We were sure there'd be loads of England fans doing the same and Friday night in Carlisle would be alright anyway. The hotel was reached in good time and we got ready for the Friday night out. Carlisle was as quite as it could possibly be and even when we asked where to go we were just told that this was it. I've since been back with a few locals and it was clear we were in the wrong spot. Settling for a kebab we went back to the hotel and got an early night ready for the big day.

Waking the next day early because we couldn't help it, in the same way as a kid does on Christmas Day, we had breakfast and set off. Unfortunately for me, Loz, had now discovered that the flags we had could double as pea shooters, if you pulled the top off the mini flag poles. I say unfortunately because I was the only one who couldn't retaliate as I was driving the bus. I therefore sustained constant attack as I drove towards Glasgow on the motorway ending up with a magazine wedged down the back of my shirt neck for protection and the inside of the windscreen plastered with chewed up paper from failed attempts to hit me. When it did hit it hurt and they even managed to hit the inside of my glasses on several occasions.

When we crossed the border there was a visible police presence as we had been advised there would be. This prevented us from carrying out the plan to plant the St. George cross next to the 'Welcome to Scotland' sign. Whilst it would have been funny it wouldn't have been worth getting into bother for, so, on we went. Every motorway junction had a police car on it, all the way to Glasgow, then, as we got nearer to Glasgow we were waved into a large car park at a service station by the police and interviewed. Are you going to the match? Once again biting our lips we said just, yes. Did we have tickets? Yes, we did and hesitating first, we told them that we were the band and it seemed to do the trick. A bit of a gamble because they could have kept us there, as they did loads of others but we were told to go on our way, for which we were grateful. Maybe our good reputation had gone before us or we just looked harmless, which of course we are. Passionate to the extreme but harmless.

The FA and ourselves were building up a great working relationship with the ticket situation and we knew we had great tickets on the back row at Hampden Park. Hampden would be another first visited ground for us to tick off. As we approached the ground we encountered the usual welcome waves that greet away fans from the locals and several welcoming parties outside pubs, which was nice. We managed to get right next to the stadium to park the mini bus which was handy because it was a little hostile to say the least, that hostility increasing the further away from the stadium you went. We were just interested in getting in as soon as possible and giving it our all for England along with the travelling support that numbered more than 10,000 that day.

Every England supporter was up for it that day. We were going to create an atmosphere for the Scots in their own back yard that they'd not witnessed before. Even in the warm-up the team looked up for the game too. Some might ask how we know. We just do, with the experience of watching matches that we and other fans have, you can just tell when everything is right.

The teams came out to a tremendous roar and lined up for the national anthems. The national anthem at the beginning of the game is every fans opportunity to demonstrate to the opposition the passion you feel for your country and we take great pride in singing as loud as possible, chest pushed out and proud to be English. If I look to the other band members they will be stood proud in exactly the same way belting out God Save the Queen. Our anthem came first being the away team to howls and whistles from the Scots who really don't like it when they have to sing it as the national anthem of the UK. We love that fact of course. The Flower of Scotland rang out next but we couldn't tell what they were saying. Then, with a knowing nod, Murray banged the drum der, der, der der der, der der der der England! It was loud, it was very loud and the Hampden crowd were stunned. We didn't stop from the start of the game to the final whistle, all of us driving each other to keep going as the sweat dripped down our bodies and Murray got more blisters. Max introduced the Great Escape, via his snare, and the English support sounded as good as it had anywhere. Another national anthem, as loud as ever and Paul Scholes bangs two goals in before half time making it even better. "Where's your famous Hampden roar?" was the impromptu chant that went up as there was as hush from the opposition support. Then, the unveiling of a St. George cross with Rangers written across the centre was greeted with a resounding cheer from the England fans this being a suggestion that Glasgow Rangers fans were supporting England, having defected.

"Keep going," was the shout down the line and we did, fuelled by adrenalin and an overwhelming desire to blow away the opposition support, which was waning. The English support that day was absolutely magnificent and we were so proud to be a part of it. We even managed to make a song up for the occasion,
"Oh you tak the High Road
and I'll tak the Low Road
and we'll be in Belgium before ye,
cos wee Paul Scholes has scored two goals
and silenced the roar at Hampden!"

At the end of the game the players came over to the terrace, behind the goal where we were all sited and applauded. They were greeted with a tremendous roar and another resounding national anthem. Once again we were totally drained but my God, it was worth every ounce of energy that we expelled.

Needless to say, the Scots weren't very happy at being out-played by the English and in a moment to cherish two kilted Scots came up to the fences that separated the fans, turned their backs to us and lifted their kilts to show their bare arses. That was the icing on the cake, how funny did they look?

The game was won and in some style but now we had the task of getting out of Glasgow, preferably alive! The minibus was parked with the England coaches so we had no problem getting away safely. On the way to the M8 we passed loads of pubs with a send off party at each one. Outside one pub two cars were turned over with the windows smashed in - whether that was normal I don't know but we didn't stop to find out.

We were happy singing the new, wee Paul Scholes song, as we joined the motorway heading south, back to England. The plan was to stop at the first service station which was only a minute or so away. The plan was good, however, the bus began to cough and splutter. There's usually miles left in them when you get to empty, surely we'd make it to the service station. No, we wouldn't. The bus came to a halt on the hard shoulder. "Bollocks!" We were still ecstatically happy but stuck on the hard shoulder with no diesel. The service station was too far away to push the bus to and it was uphill, I had an RAC membership but we thought if we could get some diesel from somewhere we'd make it to the service station, fill up and be on our way.

There was a bridge over the motorway so we thought it wouldn't be far until we found a petrol station. Leaving the others behind and in our England shirts, Murray and I climbed up the bank, along a wall and over the fence to guess which way to walk to the nearest petrol station. Asking for directions didn't seem to be the best idea but walking around a Glasgow suburb in an England shirt having just beaten Scotland 2-0 at home wasn't the best idea either. You can only imagine the looks. They were the kind of looks that give you a sense that something very nasty could happen if we didn't sort ourselves out soon. At that point a breakdown truck went past and we managed to flag him down. Quite what he said to us in his strong Glaswegian accent we didn't know but we caught the bit about, "Yous must be mad!" and "Thirteen murders in this area this year". We didn't want to make it fifteen and fortunately we'd hit lucky. The driver of the breakdown truck was a Celtic fan who explained that he, "Didn't give a toss about Scotland losing." Phew, what a relief that was. He took us to the petrol station and back to our broken down bus with the diesel. After a bit of fiddling with the engine it started up, we gave our saviour a few quid for his help and drove off. After about a hundred yards the minibus conked out again. "No!" we couldn't believe it. There was no way we were repeating the same fuel-searching experience as we did before. We'd survived the first and gained a bit of useful local knowledge about murders that had put us off, a lot. The RAC were called and got to us about forty-five minutes later. We'd been on the hard shoulder now for about two hours. The RAC did their stuff and followed us to the service station to make sure we didn't run out again as before.

I took some stick for running out of diesel, deservedly, but we were on our way south at last. "Oh, you tak the High Road and I'll tak the Low Road..................."

It was the early hours of the morning by the time we arrived home knowing that in three days time we'd be back at Wembley for the second leg of the play off and Scotland would be at Wembley again.

Times had changed since those early England v Scotland games, and there was now considerable support for England and the game was no longer classed as, 'just for the Scots'. As such, the game sold out weeks before and the Scotland support numbered just the same as any other away team at Wembley who had a section to our right.

As you might expect the Scots were in fine voice, this being their biggest game ever but we weren't having it. England were going to Holland and Belgium in 2000, not them, and we were going to finish the job that we'd started on the previous Saturday with the momentous 2-0 victory. England fans were in fine voice too with a feeling that it was party time.

For us the record company had already been on the phone saying that they were going to re-release The Great Escape, with a rapping version if we qualified. We had to get there first and England didn't start the game well at all. After thirty-nine minutes Hutchinson scored for Scotland which meant that we had to listen to, 'Doe a deer,' sung by the Scots for half an hour. David Seaman kept us in the game as all the England fans sat on the edge of their seats for the rest of the game, before finally, the ref blew his whistle and we were on our way to Holland and Belgium for Euro 2000. Scotland had their revenge but ultimately we had qualified and that was what mattered. "Yes!"

Chapter Fifteen

Once again England had qualified for a major tournament, Euro 2000 in Holland and Belgium. It was a hop, skip and jump for England fans and there was a real buzz about the nation with Kevin Keegan at the helm. There seemed to be an embracing of his cavalier style of play and maybe that was needed to win a cup competition, particularly in the knock-out stages.

Before any of the Euro games took place there were valuable friendly games to play against quality opposition, namely Argentina, Brazil and Ukraine. All the games would be at Wembley Stadium, the home of English football, certainly for all of my life and where we won the World Cup in 1966 of course. These friendlies were almost the last chance for fans to watch England in the same surroundings as all those years previously because the stadium was to be demolished to make way for a brand new state-of-the-art stadium.

The games saw the debuts of youngsters such as Heskey and Gerrard, who both impressed and gave Kevin Keegan some exciting options for the forthcoming tournament. Friendly games aren't always the best games for fans with the competitive edge missing and players often desperately trying to avoid injury and these games proved to be no exception.

We drew with our rivals Argentina 0-0, 1-1 with Brazil and beat Ukraine 2-0, the band being ever present at each game. The best for us being the friendly against Argentina because I don't think we can really have a friendly against Argentina from a fans perspective, not after the hand of God incident in '86 and Beckham's sending off in '98. The crowd were up for it too due to the history but couldn't inspire a victory.

By the time we got to Malta for the final friendly game of England's Euro 2000 preparation we had been back in the studio to record a rapping version of the Great Escape with V2, Richard Branson's record label, the same company as before having another go at what surely must be a hit. The rapper was a guy called 'Ricardo the Force' who seemed to be a great guy and good fun. No sign of any bling or guns so we were 'cool' with him. It was at the video shoot that we met rather than in the studio, such are the recording processes that you never meet half the people on any record that you make.

The video shoot involved an overnight stay in London before we met very early the next day at Tower Bridge. The record company had put us up in the Novotel just down the river from The Oval cricket ground. We had some new band members who hadn't travelled so much with us before but were very welcome to join the fold and the mad things that happened in hotels. One such new member was Ken, real name Steve Wood, who, whilst being a great guy and a superbly loud euphonium player, can appear a little boring at times, especially when espousing the virtues of disused canals. Ken is also a teacher hence Ken ....Barlow. It didn't take us long to start giving his name to TV companies as Ken Barlow and seeing it appear on the screen when he was interviewed.

On entering the hotel late at night we saw an area in the foyer that was designed to occupy the kids when guests checked in, so there were a few toys, a letter board and a one dimensional plastic dolphin in a stand. Murray and Loz set about writing rude words on the letters board as we checked in. Some highly inappropriate words were left on the board as we went to drop our stuff off in the rooms prior to meeting in the bar. They were removed before any kids could be offended the next day.

We chatted to the Irish barman and ordered some drinks until everyone arrived. Ken joined us, ordered a drink and then declared he was going to the toilet and would see us in a minute. This was our chance. There was a large plant in a massive plant pot that we could wedge behind the toilet cubical door, which strangely opened outwards. When we finally got it in place it was clear that it wasn't going to do the job. Ken who is about 6ft 5in and a big bloke would just push it out of the way. Something else was needed and then we saw it, the solid plastic dolphin from the kids area was perfect. It fitted like a glove behind the door with no room for movement at all as it wedged up to the wall. Ken could be in there for hours if desired or so we thought.

We went back to the bar laughing at the kerfuffle in the toilet, sitting down to give it about five minutes before we let him out and then we heard the biggest bang ever, a kind of piercing crack of a sound. The bang was so loud that it triggered the strangest reaction amongst all of us, we just ran for cover anywhere that we could. I ended up under a table in the dining room with Joe, our younger drummer under the next one hidden by the table cloth. Loz went behind the bar, Murray was hidden in the foyer and then Ken came round the corner with the hotel manager. Slowly we all emerged in turn from our various hiding places like naughty school boys. Myself from under the table then Joe from the next one, Loz popped up from behind the bar with the Irish barman and Murray crept in from the foyer. "What happened Ken?". What had happened was that Ken thought we were all behind the door keeping him in the toilet so him being eighteen stones plus and fancying his chances he went to the rear of the cubical and ran at the door with all his might smashing the plastic dolphin into smithereens and creating this almighty bang in the process.

The manager was a little disbelieving as you might expect but soon came round when we apologised and he realised no harm was meant. Our apology was accompanied by a £150 payment towards the kids' toy area and a new dolphin.

The next day we were up early for the video with Murrays first words being, "F****** ridiculous," which it was of course. Eighteen stone man smashes dolphin in hotel toilet, you couldn't write it.

The video crew were there at Tower Bridge on time as we were and as was the trend at the time we found ourselves on the top deck of a bus travelling around London playing to a record, that we could hardly hear, with Ricardo rapping away. Several innocent bystanders wondered what was going on as the bus passed by and various shouts went out to them and the crew got the usual shock treatment. Remarkably, the finished result was quite good musically and visually giving us high hopes of this particular single being a hit. We were still enjoying the sponsorship of Admiral, showing off their kit in the video and Dr Martens boots too. The record was launched with all the publicity it had before, Soccer AM appearances, local ITV Calender and Look North news programmes. For the ITV programme we had to go to Leeds for a tea-time slot. On the way there we managed to lose Bram somehow, who was in a different car. Time was against us and the studio could wait no longer, we had to appear on the show, they had put us in the studio garden because we were so loud inside the studio. We lined up in our normal formation as the show's floor manager counted us down to start playing 3-2-1, just as he got to -1 Bram appeared on the end of the line from nowhere. Note perfect we finished the piece to tremendous laughter and a rather hurried explanation from Bram that he'd been all over Leeds looking for us after we lost him. We managed to get home without losing anyone.

The Malta trip cost us a fortune and coupled to the expense of Euro 2000 we were feeling the pinch when a saviour appeared in the BBC who offered us a deal to do a documentary of the band at Euro 2000. Some of the lads couldn't afford to go so that helped with their fares and ticket costs. When we got to Malta we found it to be like England, with sun, but without the tackiness. Driving was on the left, the signs in English and the same as ours. Give Way was an inverted triangle just like at home. Having been made very welcome by the Maltese we entered the stadium that was not much more than you might find in non-league over here, in fact not even that good. They had obviously borrowed a PA system from somewhere with really large speakers on the ground pointing towards the stand. It was literally unbearable to stay in the stand with the speakers booming out but once you were in you were trapped and tortured with this deafening sound. Such was the pain that any small nook or cranny had been found by fans to shield the sound. The snack bar was packed because it was under the stand and away from the sound but even there the ground was vibrating. Numbers were down slightly on the normal travelling support but were bolstered by ex- pats and we managed to pull off a 2-1 win which was a good result for Malta, who we were expected to trounce. The game left us with the strange feeling of being disappointed as we travelled home, even though we'd won.

Nine days on was when it mattered, the start of Euro 2000 in Holland and Belgium and England against Portugal in Eindhoven. Due to the various work commitments of the band members we opted to fly in and out of Holland for the game, which isn't a problem as we've done it regularly. They are well used to us at Schipol airport and we to them as we seem to play Holland as much as we play Poland. Along with the BBC we hired a van from the airport and drove to Eindhoven for the game. When we arrived in the city, having made sure that we'd put enough diesel in the tank, it was clear that an English invasion had taken place.

The usual taking over of the city squares by the fans had happened, with St.George cross flags draped everywhere that they could fit. Each flag labelled with the place name or team of the owner and maybe their own names. There are certain flags that you recognise as regulars from all over the country, Brentford, Bristol, Treeton and Norwich being some of them. Surprisingly to some, there is an absence of flags claiming allegiance to England's most successful league teams but, when you think that proper fans of those clubs have to attend seventy five plus games, at home and abroad, it may be understandable that they're not there, and the rest of us, that don't travel Europe with our clubs, are.

It was clear again that the English support was going to outnumber the Portuguese and that was confirmed once we entered the stadium. The Philips stadium is, as you may expect, being owned by an electrical company, quite technically advanced, with one of the best PA systems and big screens anywhere. It wasn't loud enough to mask the noise coming from the England fans though which was booming out from the terraces in anticipation of the team's arrival. The national anthem before the game made the hairs on the back of your neck stand up, each England fan demonstrating their passion and support for the team in the unique way that the singing of the national anthem demands. What must the players think out there on the pitch if it fills our chests with pride on the terraces?

Nine of us made the trip over to the game, Murray, Bram, Julie, Max, Brian, Adolf, Ken, Joe and myself which was more than enough to get the whole place bouncing and bouncing it was when we took the lead after only three minutes through that man again Paul Scholes. The atmosphere got even better when we extended the lead after eighteen minutes, Steve McManaman scoring. Portugal were a good side with class players like Figo, Pinto and Gomes in their side, not that we cared, at 2-0 up we were cruising.

The problem with class players is that they're good. Good enough to fight back from a 2-0 reverse? Well, yes, they were. Two of Portugal's class players scored bringing them level by half time and the pressure was back on us to get the crowd going again and the team to try and pluck a victory from somewhere in the second half.

By this time we had introduced a now familiar tradition of the fans national anthem at the beginning of the second half. All regular England fans are aware that this happens and we all gave a rousing rendition to inspire the team for the second half. It was a cracking contest but unfortunately Portugal scored on sixty minutes and try as we might on and off the field we just couldn't get that equaliser or even go on to win it. The result was disappointing, however, we knew from previous tournaments that all was not lost if you lose the first game, other games were to come against our old rivals Germany and Romania.

Back in the hire car and back to Schipol airport to catch the plane to England with the BBC in tow, filming. The usual antics of passport and boarding card stealing took place before we boarded the plane home. Barely had we touched down and had time to say hello to our other halves than we were back at the airport ready to fly back to Belgium, BBC in tow again, car hire and off to Charleroi. Charleroi is a small, historic Belgium town with a very traditional main square. Whilst driving around, it soon became apparent that this is where the England fans had congregated so we looked to park up as close as possible to that area for a number of reasons.

One was that Adam Black, who was still helping us out with sponsorship deals, where possible, had managed to get a deal with Tango that involved us carrying a backdrop around and playing in front of it wherever we were. The idea being it would help fund the trip.

Another reason was that we'd been asked to go on Radio 5, who were situated on the fourth floor of what seemed to be the Town Hall, overlooking the main square. And thirdly, that's where we wanted to be, along with all the other fans because we had another task to perform at the stadium later.

We parked in a very convenient underground car park that was right under the main square and all piled into the lift, complete with what had become known as the black coffin on wheels. This was the box that held the back drop that nobody wanted to have to carry to and from the sites that we played at. It was painful but had to be done. Once we'd all squeezed into the lift, three floors below ground level we pressed the button to go up, the doors closed then nothing happened, nothing other than the doors stayed closed and we didn't go anywhere. Looking around we saw a sign in French that said maximum eight people and another next to it that said the car park closed on a Friday at 5 p.m. and didn't open until Monday morning. It was 4 p.m. on the Friday and we had nine of us, all the instruments and the black coffin crammed into the lift and were stuck. The last thing we needed was to be stuck in there all weekend and miss the match into the bargain. There was a speaker in the lift with a button to press in case of emergency so we pressed it and got two French speaking blokes who we didn't understand but they seemed to think it was funny that we were all stuck in this six foot square box in red hot temperatures.

It was at this point that Bram, who is usually the most reverend of us all, went berserk! He shouted at the speaker, as we all did in fairness, some choice words too, he then began to kick and pull at the doors in an attempt to free us and him from our very unpleasant and frightening ordeal. Our conclusion was that Bram must have been a little claustrophobic or more than a little as it turned out. Fortunately, somehow, after about ten minutes the lift started to move and we reached the square and fresh air, much to everyone's relief. We did our bit in front of the back drop and then Murray and I went to the temporary Radio 5 studio on the fourth floor of the Town

Hall type building in the square. When we got to the studio it was just an attic-type room with a couple of presenters and their broadcast equipment and fabulous double French doors that opened up onto the square below.

When the inevitable request to play something came we knew just what to do. Opening the double doors Murray started a drum roll and as loud as possible I blasted the national anthem out over the thousands of England fans below. Immediately they all joined in producing a fantastic display of English passion for the locals, who had clearly not seen anything like it before, nor for that matter had the Radio 5 presenters who stood aghast. With a very satisfying look on our faces the interview finished there, there was no topping it. We love it when something like that happens, to be able to share in those moments is absolutely priceless.

The rest of the guys had a knowing smile when we got back to them, having heard what had happened. The black coffin was packed up quickly, as we didn't have much time left to get to the stadium, even earlier than normal. The reason was that we were booked to play on the pitch before the game - now that truly was f****** ridiculous. The plan was that Ricardo the Force would fly over and together with us would mime on the pitch to our record that would be piped through the speakers. We arrived on time at the stadium but there was no sign of Ricardo and then word came that he hadn't made it due to a flight delay, so, Adam Black's mate stepped in, threw a St.George flag around himself and on the pitch we went.

The tunnel through which we entered the stadium was at the German end and they applauded us as did the England fans when we took our position on the pitch. The teams were warming up on the pitch so we were there with David Beckham, Michael Owen and the rest of the guys dancing around like idiots but resisting the attempt to have a kick about. The stand-in lead singer was doing well thrusting the microphone right into his mouth so that nobody noticed. Our performance culminated in all of us kneeling down on the 18 yard line facing the England fans with hands aloft bowing in appreciation which went down really well and the same gesture came back along with gratefully received applause.

Now the Germans, who had applauded us onto the field before, had seen all of this going on and maybe figured out what it was all about and our exit from the pitch and back down the tunnel at their end was very different to our arrival. Nothing was thrown, other than abuse, and that rather courteously in English, they're always showing off those Germans.

There was plenty of time to get back to our position in the stand, the path to which went down the players' tunnel and round to our section. As we got there the teams had finished their warm up and came down the tunnel as we came up. A privilege for us, by chance, and we'd also managed to see and acknowledge Victoria Beckham on the way around. It was David Beckham that took our attention and that of the media too because as we crossed at the end of the tunnel some fans began to hurl abuse at him, insulting anything they could think of, including his wife and family. These idiots thought it was the thing to do following the sending off in the World Cup two years earlier. We were disgusted. There was no call for anything like that to be said to any player, never mind one of our best players without whom England wouldn't have qualified and has given everything for his country. There was a media storm about the incident which took place before we kicked off in a really important game for the country. What absolute idiots.

The game was to come and as ever the England v Germany clash has that special something that gives it an edge. The last thing we needed was penalties of course and we were buoyed by the fact that we were playing in the famous red shirts as we did in the 1966 final.

The stand where the bulk of the England fans were sited was behind the goal. A two-tier stand, we made our way to the top tier and entering the stand found that it was unbelievably steep, like no stand that we'd ever been in before and we have been in a few. Not only was it steep but the concrete slabs that made up the steps had gaps in between them through which you could see straight down the hundreds of feet below to the ground. This led to quite a bit of humour, especially close to kick off when those fans who like to maximise drinking time arrived. One fan entered the stadium and immediately began to crawl up the gangway steps on his hands and knees, commando style, for fear of falling down the stand, exclaiming that he'd come to a football match and wasn't geared up for mountaineering!

By the time kick-off came the whole place was bouncing and I mean literally bouncing. We started to play a little earlier than normal this being a match against Germany and so critical a game. Everyone was up for it as you would expect but we realised just how much when we saw that the floodlights that protruded from the stand over the pitch were bouncing up and down in time to the chants coming from the stand. So much so that the light was flickering on the pitch as the noise, like never before, was deafeningly loud and blasted away any sound that may have come from the Germans.

Fans and band never stopped throughout the game with the stand bouncing continually and I swear that when Alan Shearer scored on fifty three minutes I thought the whole stand was coming down. Several fans went tumbling down the stand over the seats which didn't surprise us as we all jumped for joy hugging anyone and everyone.

All those times that we'd lost on penalties, Euro '96 and all, when Gazza just didn't connect with the ball as it flew across the goal had been parked in our memories and this was our time. The England fans really made the most of it and although we'd heard of this concept called dynamic excitation, we'd never really witnessed it like we were then. The concept is that a sustained rhythm can make buildings vibrate and the Charleroi stand certainly did that night.

We left the stadium still playing two songs that were more popular than others, 'We're not going home,' to the tune of 'Knees up Mother Brown,' simply because we weren't going home and, 'We'll meet again,' a Vera Lynn's classic.

In Kevin Keegan's post match interview we were extremely pleased to hear him go over the top in praise of the fans for the noise that was generated that night. Not only that he confirmed that when he looked over to the stand that he could see the floodlights bouncing up and down, unbelievable.

It was our first victory over Germany since the World Cup and it was so sweet to taste the success. We only needed a draw now against Romania to go through to the knockout stages with the game taking place at the same ground, Charleroi, in Belgium. Would the stand be able to take it?

The three days between the games were crammed with TV and radio interview as the country went football mad. The record company had been on the phone again to say that they had had unprecedented demand for the record and that if we beat Portugal it would definitely go to the top ten or even higher. We'd done the boomerang trip home and back to Belgium for the game against Romania and arrived back in the now familiar town of Charleroi.

There was no performance before the kick off to deal with, the first one was probably enough, so we did our mountaineering early to get in position at the back of the stand ready to make it bounce again. There had been a small amount of trouble previously in the town centre so it was best keeping well away and concentrating on getting in position. The support for the team was good again with about ten thousand fans making the journey to, hopefully, watch England progress towards the quarter finals.

Unfortunately Romania took the lead after twenty-two minutes, Nigel Martyn having no chance of stopping the shot come across that went in off the post. That signalled a rallying call from us and the fans and the response came from the team. By half time we had managed to get ourselves in front via a Shearer penalty and wonder kid, Michael Owen, who was maturing well by now. That was more like it and the half time chat revolved around tentative arrangements for the quarter final because even a draw would take us through. Football, being as it is, we knew not to count our chickens and within three minutes of the restart Romania had equalised 2-2. This scoreline would still be enough for us to go through so no panic yet. Eighty minutes gone and we were playing away as loud as possible knowing that we were almost there. Just survive for ten minutes and we're home and dry. Eighty-five minutes gone, all is well, more songs and more nail biting. Eighty-six minutes, eighty-eight, more 'Great Escape' to calm the nerves of us all. Then eighty-nine minutes and Romania, who would go through if they won, mounted an attack and with their player, Moldovan, appearing to be going nowhere in the area right in front of us Phil Neville brought him down to concede a penalty.

"No! No! No! No! You tosser Neville! Why? Why?". I was distraught, as were all the England fans. How the hell had we managed to go behind, get level, go in front and then throw it all away. These were good players, good players didn't do that.

We just sat there heads in hands. It was too much for others who were in tears. Some fans vented their anger at the team but most couldn't find the energy, such was the depression that had engulfed us all. As we left the stadium many fans said, "Well done lads," and we thanked them, praising them for their efforts too. We don't seek any adulation at all, we just do what we do like other fans sing in support of the team. That said, it is nice when fellow fans show their appreciation and very humbling. Football fans don't do that kind of thing lightly and it is appreciated.

Flying back to England we were bemoaning the fact that, 'it had put paid to the record then' and how we should be able to sue Phil Neville for loss of earnings, having missed out on a top ten hit, when we met the guy from Umbro. Umbro were England's kit manufacturer and their man put things into perspective regarding losses when he said that they had made thousands more shirts shipped them all over the country ready for the boom in demand that there was sure to be. They'd spent thousands on new stock and distribution that would now take however long to sell, if at all.

That's the gamble I suppose, for us records are just a bonus and a laugh, the main thing is supporting the team, for him it was his living and hundreds of other jobs. It gave us an insight into a different sphere and we wondered how many others were affected, there must be thousands, never mind all us millions who were gutted at the result.

The end of the tournament from an England point of view meant the end of the BBC documentary. Richard the producer had done a great job and was less intrusive than the previous 'Cutting Edge' documentary at the France World Cup. The documentary went out on the BBC on our return, which closed off the tournament for us. The record producer and label MD nearly committed suicide as, once again, the Gods had been against us for making 'The Great Escape' a hit. We did forgive Phil Neville but it took a few years.

Chapter Sixteen

Strange things started to happen when we got home. Strange in that we received numerous calls to appear on different shows and at different events, in addition to all those mad ones that we'd been involved in previously. We also found ourselves doing some pretty daft things ourselves as we entered this media-led world we knew nothing of.

For example, our dedication to our team, Sheffield Wednesday and to England meant that we couldn't miss a game for either. When the teams are scheduled to play on the same day it creates a problem but is not insurmountable, if they're both at home. One such occasion was when England's next away game in Paris, playing France and Wednesday's away game at Watford fell on the same day. Knowing well in advance that this was potentially a problem for us I asked the club secretary at Wednesday if there was any chance that the game would be called off due to international call ups.

"No, absolutely no chance, we don't have any and Watford had one".

"Will it be moved to allow fans to travel to the game or watch it on TV?"

"No".

OK, so we knew where we stood. The game at Watford kicked off at 3 p.m. and the game in Paris we knew would be a late night kick off. The only way to do it would be to hire a plane, a private jet, that would do it.

Never underestimate the ability and will of a football fan to get to watch his team. There are many cases of madness in this field and we were about to enter it. After a bit of research I found out that a company called, Metropolitan Aviation, could fly us to France in a private ten seater jet from Stamford Airport, just inside the M25 and not too far from Watford, and get us there for the kick off. The cost was, "f****** ridiculous," but there was no other way. We left it until the last minute and after checking a final time with our club secretary, who again confirmed that the Wednesday/Watford game would definitely go ahead, so we booked the plane.

The international squads were announced a week in advance of the games and guess what, there wasn't three internationals in either team, and that was the ruling to trigger postponement of the league fixture, but the announcement came that the Watford v Wednesday game had been postponed. Smashin! We'd spent all that money when we could have hopped over the channel for a fraction of the cost and we couldn't get a refund at such short notice. Nice one.

The benefit of the postponement was that we could now take our time and travel over at whatever time we wanted. Stamford airport was actually a field, with no customs or shops, a few plane spotters but that was it. It was a very different way of travelling to what we'd been used to. Each of us had to be weighed which brought a few cheers when the truth was known about one or two members' weights. Julie was a little conscious of her weight and point blank refused to let anyone know what she weighed.

With our pilot and crew calling us, sir, it certainly was a very different experience. On signing the guest book we noticed that the last person to use the plane was Frank Bruno, now he's used to being weighed.

A few jokes were cracked about our pilot being a woman on her first mission before we fearlessly climbed aboard. There was a scramble for the plush leather seats and poor old Max missed out having to sit on the closed toilet seat, for most of the journey, behind a curtain with only the instruments for company.

The flight itself was interesting because smaller planes fly at a lower altitude giving a far better view of what's going on below. Once we'd got used to the bobbing up and down of the small plane and the pilot had suffered more ribbing about her first flight, we settled down to watch the various ships crossing the channel, which were far more than you'd think. The scary thing was that other light aircraft fly at the same altitude in the opposite direction and whilst I'm sure the pilots knew what they were doing, to the layman, i.e. us, there were a few clenched bottom moments.

We made a perfect landing at Charles de Gaul Airport. We were in a different part of the airport and simply walked through a building, no customs, thanked our pilots and got into the waiting cars, that were included in the package. We could get used to this I'm sure, the only problem being the price!

After all this the game was a bit of a let-down despite it being against World Cup winners, France, in their own back yard, it was a typical friendly match and the French crowd didn't even sing, not that we could hear anyway given our usual performance. I must say that their national anthem is a belter but we all think of Cantona now when we hear it, the famous ex-Sheffield Wednesday forward (for one week anyway).

After the match we walked around for hours trying to flag down a cab. This seems to be a problem for us wherever we are in the world - we can never get a taxi and is something that Bram can well do without it, we can all well do without. Paris was one of the worst places ever for this. Eventually we did get a cab back to the hotel and after a good night's sleep decided to have a walk on the Champs el Lyses. We took the Metro, very quickly realising that there was a wonderful echo in the underground. Someone started singing the tune to the Wool advert that was on TV at the time, a sort of chanting monk's type song and it didn't take long before we were in full voice and harmony with this fabulous echo coming back at us from down the various tunnels.

The locals stopped short of joining in but offered the odd smile; deduce from that what you may.

Walking down from the Arc de Triumph I got a phone call from the pilot of the plane.

"What time would you like to fly back sir?"

"I thought you told us that?" I said.

We really weren't used to this treatment, it was usually more like: check in two hours before we leave, become bored and buy some rubbish before we eventually board the plane. After a brief discussion I asked, "How about 4 p.m?"

"That's fine sir, we'll send the cars to the hotel for that time".

No problem getting a cab there then.

The flight back was just as good as the one out to France; we landed on the field at Stamford and without any hassle from non-existent customs were in our cars five minutes later and on the way home. A very enjoyable one-off trip leaving us thinking, if only, but no, we're better off with everyone else really, we'll leave that as a one-off.

Another form of transport that we became familiar with a little closer to home was an open-top bus. There was an article in The Star newspaper, the local Sheffield evening paper, about an open top bus being put up for auction. The bus was part of lots from an ex-Sheffield United director's company that had been repossessed. He had reportedly bought it so that if Sheffield United ever won the cup or got promoted they had a bus to ride on through the city. Various opinions exist on that possibility but that fact alone was enough of a motivator to spur us on to go to the auction and bid for the bus.

The bidding started at £300 for the 1949 Route Master III so Murray and I had a bid. It must be worth that in scrap was our justification for this mindless moment and the idea that we would use it to go to games in. I had a class one HGV license so could drive the bus (but with no paying passengers) and knew enough companies from my time selling HGV's that would help maintain it, so maybe it wasn't so daft to bid. The final bid of £500 was ours so we'd bought the bus and just burst out laughing when the hammer fell.

I got some help from Askey's Transport in Hillsborough to get the old thing going and drove it down from Park Head in Sheffield where it resided, down Ecclesall Road towards a roundabout at the bottom of the hill at Hunters Bar. The bus hadn't been used for years and actually had Hull City stickers all over it for some reason which had to be removed before the drive of course but it was the brakes I was worried about. The mechanics weren't like anything I'd come across before with no power steering, strange three-speed automatic gearbox and pull up windows. I had to use two hands to pull on one side of the steering wheel to turn the bus, the brakes needed two feet to slow it down at the same time as trying to steer it round the roundabout. Once I'd managed that I knew I was OK as the rest of the journey was along the flat or uphill.

I then enjoyed the trip, hooting at interested passers-by and enjoying the nods and waves from fellow double-decker bus drivers travelling in the other direction as I'd become an honorary member for a day. When I looked in my mirrors I saw that there was a trail of leaves emitting from the top deck. The bus had been parked under trees for a number of years and the leaves were two feet deep on the top deck. So as I travelled along it was like having a confetti trail behind me. Best of all though was that for once in my life I could travel down the bus lane without fear of prosecution and I can thoroughly recommend it.

The bus was filmed for a feature by Sky Sports who somehow got word of its existence but unfortunately it never made it to the road because of time and money constraints. The irony was that we sold the bus, for more money than we bought it, to a hospitality company who later, having restored it, hired it to Sheffield United to parade the team through the city when they won promotion later that year. I suppose what goes around comes around is the fitting phrase.

About the same time in the late nineties I made my BBC Radio 4 debut with the composer of The Great Escape, Alma Bernstein. Radio 4 was off limits really for me, as a sports fan there's not much there plus having been forced to listen to it by my Mum at the breakfast table when I was younger it didn't appeal. However, on the phone-in show I was with Alma who was very kind and quite pleased that we had adopted his tune for a terrace anthem. Obviously we didn't know who was going to phone in and I remember we had to endure, disgruntled of Tunbridge Wells, who thought the tune should be left alone and not used as a ghastly football chant and, although she wouldn't take it from me, Alma's word was accepted when he basically said he was fine with it so chill out.

The media world also introduced us to the PR agency. One such agency contacted us to play at, The Stoop, in London at a rugby game to promote Fosters lager. They were paying and we needed the money so we found ourselves labelled up in the amber nectar clothing at a London Bronco's v Wakefield game parading round the ground on a Sunday afternoon. We were totally unaware but the locals living next to the stadium had objected to the council about the noise that the new Sunday afternoon rugby games were generating. The speakers at the stadium were quite loud pre-match with the music blaring out and the various activities going on but not really any worse than other places. I suppose it's different if you're not used to it.

The reason we were aware that the locals had objected was that after we had paraded up and down in front of the stand a few times a delegation from Richmond Council approached us, in the company of Radio 5 who were recording the whole thing, to serve a noise abatement order on us. The guy with the legal papers had just started his speech when the ground began to shake and the noise above our heads was so loud that we crouched down to get away from it. Concorde was flying over and with Heathrow not very far away at all it felt like we could touch the plane. The Stoop was clearly on a flight path and there couldn't possibly be anything louder than Concorde in your back garden. The Radio 5 reporter just looked at us and we at him with a knowing smile as the council guy struggled to be heard above Concorde as he continued to serve the papers on the rugby club, picking us as their representatives. It was a total farce, nonetheless a memorable moment indeed.

That was a brief encounter with rugby but our relationship with Rugby League in particular became more permanent when we were asked to play for the Leeds Rhinos in the late nineties. The area wasn't so strange to me having worked in West Yorkshire and Leeds in particular. We were, and still are of course, football people. There is a kind of divide between South and West Yorkshire, West Yorkshire is rugby, South Yorkshire isn't. Sheffield Eagles would probably disagree but for me I'd never really seen and been involved in a rugby match properly until then. Not the same for Murray, I might add. There is a big Sheffield/Leeds rivalry in football and many other things actually but not in rugby, so we didn't have split allegiances at all as far as we were concerned, not that we'd shout about it in Sheffield.

In Rugby League the atmosphere is completely different to that of football, certainly friendlier and we were made very welcome in the South Stand at Headingly after not really knowing what to expect. The fans were and still are superb, helping us to quickly establish ourselves as the South Stand Band and with them, we began to create what is now the best atmosphere anywhere in the Super League.

Our next bizarre contact was from an events company involved with the Rugby Union at Twickenham. They asked us to play for England as the band in the stand at the Rugby World Cup in 1999. It was very different to football and Rugby League - the two codes aren't supposed to cross they say. The fans are incredibly different too, it is true that Union is a more upper class pastime, but not necessarily better.

Before the game we were assembled in the green room, waiting for the game to start, when we came across two guys in the corner of the room. One was sat on the floor with his head in his hands and the other stood next to him.
"Alright?"
"Alright", came the reply.
"Where you from?" we asked as the normal ice breaker.
"Manchester".
"Oh, Sheffield".
We were both northern so that was enough of a bond on this occasion with us being in upper crust London. The guy standing was clearly looking after the one on the floor so we asked, "What's up with him?"
"Oh he's got to sing the British National Anthem and 'Barcelona' before kick-off and he's shitting himself".

In an attempt to rid his fears we had a word with him to the affect of, "Don't worry pal there's nothing to it, you just have to go out there like we do and, 'give it some pasty," you'll be alright".

The guy on the floor was only Russell Watson! He was in the early part of his career and of course it was nothing like what we had to do. His was a major performance and everything had to be right not only for those in the stadium but for millions on TV too. There's no wonder he was nervous. Whether our chat worked or not, who knows, but his performance was faultless. Our performance however took a little adaption before it worked, the new crowd not being used to a band in the stand or indeed to singing much at all. We had to give them what they wanted which was simply, Swing Low Sweet Chariots and a bit of drumming which seemed to go down well in the end. It was a great experiment in crowd culture for us with the lads having a great deal of fun, fitting in, shall we say. We return to Twickenham for the Sevens tournament once a year but not for the regular England Rugby Union games.

The next thing we knew we were at Loftus Road, home of QPR but not for football, it was Rugby Union again as this was the home of Wasps at the time. They put us in the stand behind the posts at one end, an upper tier on our own with the exception of two mascot Wasps. When Wasps scored we would run up and down the stand with the Wasp mascots, just because we could. The lasting memory being the adoption of the Ince song or Booth song if you're a Wednseday fan, falling straight in place at Wasps. It was there that one of the best come-back lines was thought of when a Gloucester fan said, "I'm going to shove that drum up your arse!" to Murray. He was met with, "Don't think it'd fit pal but we'd get it in your mouth no problem!"

Other bizarre occurrences included being involved in the Coca Cola, 'Eat, Sleep and Drink Football' adverts filming us all over Sheffield and using about two seconds of it in the advert as they normally do. Still on the drinks front a chain of pubs hired us to develop a chant about their company with their employees in a training day at Villa Park. The resulting chants had to be sung on the terraces by the employees at the end of the day to an empty stadium. Other worker training days included a World Cup day with the Post Office working with England legend, Peter Shilton. These working days are OK as long as you remember your mouthpiece. Al, one of our euphonium players, forgot his at Villa, requiring a quick trip by cab to get one from a Birmingham music shop.

The best one for forgetting a mouthpiece was Brian on a trip to London. We spent hours on our phone (not Brian's) and travelling around in the car before we finally found a replacement of the right size, which was important because it was Brian who could play properly. When we got to the shop he tried to get the mouthpiece on 'appro' (approval), meaning he would get us to drive him back after the event and say it was no good for him, thus the whole exercise cost us a fortune and him nothing. That was Brian. Very good player but tight? As a duck's.   That said, poor old Brian got picked on sometimes a little too much, although he didn't help himself and made it easy for the lads to do so. Despite having no reason he was vainer than he should be and we discovered that the tuft of hair at the front of his head when tweaked a little looked like the guy from the group, Prodigy. This was done repeatedly to the shout of, 'I am the fire starter!' Not bad for a sixty year old. Another annoyance that we couldn't get our heads around was that he insisted that he didn't like Pizza. I ask you? You can have anything on a pizza, so when we'd established that he liked tomatoes and dough there was no excuse for him. Everywhere we went, home and abroad, we purposely headed for a pizza restaurant. Brian even had his own song called, "Don't like pizza" and featuring some of his famous quotes like, "it's always you," aimed at Murray.

Another time, when perhaps what happened shouldn't have, was when we were coming back from Wembley after a game and we 'd just got level with junction 29 of the M1 where Brian gets dropped off. Brian forgot to tell us so just at the point that was too far past the turning he shouted, "Stop!" We wondered what had happened but Brian said, "it's my turn off". There followed a barrage of abuse like, "silly old bugger", as we pulled up on the hard shoulder thinking it was an emergency. "Right, get out then". It was either get out or go up to the next junction and turn round, which no one fancied, so Brian got out and clambered up the grass bank to the traffic island above and across to where his wife was waiting to pick him up. Lord knows what she said but we'd have loved to be a fly on the wall as she asked where all the mud came from.

Yet another classic Brian moment happened when the same events company that hired us for Twickenham hired us for the Carling Cup Final at Wembley between Tottenham and Leicester City. Again we were waiting in our designated room in one of the old Wembley hangers near the stadium when we noticed a microphone on a stand in the room. We found that it connected to the really large room next door, so, larking around we took it in turns to pretend to be pop stars with our best impression of whomever. When Brian went up to the microphone stand to be Frank Sinatra we turned it on and it boomed out next door. What we didn't know as that not only was it booming out in the room next door but it was booming out all over Wembley. "And now the end is near, and so I face, the final curtain". Stewards came running from everywhere. One said, "do you know what you've done?" We'd no idea, time for my best diplomacy again.

The event itself was something else. There were ten of us in the band that day and we had to split into two groups to orchestrate a battle of the fans. Five of us at the Tottenham end and the other five at the Leicester end. We'd never been on the Wembley pitch and to walk out there in front of a full house was amazing, in fact, as I said to Murray when we were walking out onto the pitch, "This is f****** ridiculous!" And it was, we played two songs each to our respective fan groups alternately and each duly joined in and then we marched off, they even applauded us which is an unusual happening for us. At least we could tick that box of playing on the pitch at Wembley.

In one of the pizza restaurants (that Brian didn't like) there was one of the funniest and most memorable moments in band history. Strange then that there's disagreement as to which country we were in, Sweden or Finland but it was definitely a Pizza Hut. The story involved a young drummer, Joe. Joe, to say the least, was a little naive. We pretended, on one occasion, to be sending a prostitute to his hotel room to give him his first sexual experience, resulting in his pacing up and down the shared room all night waiting for the knock on the door, much to the amusement of the other occupants. Another time, when he became nicknamed Joe Strummer, was when Loz, in his own unique way, was able to eek out of him his masturbation frequency which he said was "Seven".

Loz said, "Seven, not bad in a week?"

"Oh no," said Joe............... "a day".

"Bloody hell, Joe!"

You can only imagine the reaction of seven lads hearing that news, it was sheer gold to us. There followed a full investigation not only then but it became a full ongoing investigation every time we met up when the sport was to get Joe's latest confession of where and when he'd managed it, some unbelievable places. Put it this way, I wouldn't have wanted to be a student sharing his house. This aside, the memorable incident I referred to earlier was in the Scandinavian Pizza Hut when we were all sat down at the table waiting for our meal to come. Joe, being away from home and in student accommodation for the first time had let his personal hygiene slip and his clothes clearly weren't getting washed as often as they should. We told him in our own way that he stank and needed a wash. We sent him to the washroom that we could see from our table, with instruction to get a full wash from top to toe as he was putting us off our meal.

Joe was a great lad with an infectious chuckle and very talented on the drum and piano but as I said previously, naive. Sensing an opportunity, Murray went to the wash room with Joe to give him a hand.

197

"Come on Joe I'll give you a hand, let me hold your clothes". Joe duly obliged and handed Murray all his clothes except his underpants. No sooner had this happened than Murray was back at our table with a pile of Joe's clothes sat on the chair where Joe should be. The funny part came when several unsuspecting customers had gone to the toilet and Joe had to hide in the cubicle each time. Joe's head popped out of the door on several occasions with a look of desperation followed by a knowing laugh, he knew it wasn't going to happen, the clothes weren't coming back. Then the piece de resistance, in a desperate attempt to get his clothes back Joe emerged from the toilet, head popping out first followed by his half naked body with the black bin liner from the toilet bin pinned to each of his nipples by the thumb of each hand. Well, the site was enough to have the whole restaurant in uproar and we were in stitches. He made it to the table, grabbed his clothes and ran. We never did find out if he managed to wash. Joe certainly was a good lad but shortly after that he got a girl friend and we haven't seen him since. One can only imagine...............

One of the most frequently shown appearances we made was when we were filmed for, '100 Greatest Films'. We were there to comment on, 'The Great Escape' and it seems they roll the show out at every Bank Holiday because I always get texts saying, 'Just seen you on TV. When was it filmed? Looks like you've put on weight'. When we watched it back we were the next to comment on the film after Richard Attenborough which we regarded as a real privilege, even though we didn't have anything to do with it, to follow such a legendary actor made us quite proud.

Another mad occurrence was when we were invited to enter a team into the V festival 5-a-side tournament that took place in Reading. This was another strange arena that we entered with backstage passes and VIP access along with all the bands that were playing - I'd no idea who they were. The football was interesting, we played teams that included, Vernon Kaye and another that included, Take That's, Mark Owen, both of whom were great lads. Football and music you see the two things that cross all boundaries.

We knew that we weren't a bad side with most of us playing regularly at a good standard. Adolf has been a professional, I'm not bad even if I say so myself and Murray too has played at a decent standard so we found ourselves through to the final against Arsenal's academy. Arsenal were managed by a childhood hero of ours, Brian Hornsby, who played in the famous Sheffield Wednesday side that drew four times with Arsenal in the FA Cup before finally losing, even though we were a Third Division side at the time and they were top of the first. We gave it our shot but lost 2-1 to the young pros from Arsenal. I hate losing. The whole experience was lightened by the, and I mean the, legend that is Stuart Hall. Stuart had been hired to commentate on the games in the way that only he can do and the whole day was made all the better for his involvement. The sight of him on top of his scaffolding tower in between the pitches, in the pouring rain, laughing his socks off as he did in, 'It's a Knockout' years ago is a gem of a memory. We even made up a song for him, that being, 'He's Stuart Hall, he's Stuart Hall" to the tune of, 'He's on the ball', needless to say he loved it and we did too, great day.

At another 5-a-side tournament in London the opportunity presented itself for pay back. This was a tournament that Adam Black got us involved in and we'd been drawn against........Keith Allen's side. The game lasted ten minutes and it was ten minutes of sheer pleasure. Keith Allen was in goal and as mouthy on the pitch as he is off it. How sweet it was then for us to put four goals past him, including one through his legs, and they had a man carried off the pitch, don't know how that happened but it was fair to say that they suddenly became a little sheepish after a few minutes of the game and some people just aren't up for a challenge. That was a tournament that we won.

The early years of the band coincided with the launch of the film, The Full Monty, filmed in Sheffield, in fact some of it in our immediate area and all of the film sites we were familiar with. It was fitting then that a premiere of the film would take place in Sheffield. What a great night that was with many celebrities turning out from stage, screen, sport and other arms of showbiz. One memory was seeing Chris Waddle and our mate, Chris Kamara, sing Mustang Sally with Def Leopard whilst dancing on a chair with Helen Chamberlain. The party went on into the early hours and longer in some cases and by the time we'd finished we'd met most of the cast of Coronation Street and Emmerdale and even the Dream Boys! (didn't do much for us though).

Meeting celebs became a bit of a sport, especially for Loz, who would turn each situation into a farce as only he can. Celebs included Gary Newman, David Essex and once when we were waiting to go on Ian Wright's, 'Friday Night is Alright' show, Loz excelled himself. Waiting in the cafe at ITVs Upper Ground studio in London Loz noticed the news reader, Alistair Burnett, walking towards us. As he got level Loz said, 'Alistair?' at a volume level that he could have heard or not. He heard and there followed one of those moments where Loz shook his hand and poor Alistair did his best to make conversation thinking that he should know this person but clearly didn't. Loz being Loz kept the conversation going as long as possible and let it go just before he would have been rumbled with a little help from us. There then comes the silent pause before we all crack up.

Ian Wright was great, being familiar with us from his time in an England shirt. On the show with us were Gregg Rusedski, E17 and Caprice but also The Manic Street Preachers, who they really shouldn't have put us next to in the dressing room. We weren't exactly next to them, just the other side of a folding door, which made it easier for 'friendly' English/Welsh verbal banter to be projected through the gaps in the doors. No harm done. Meeting Gregg Rusedski reminded us of the time when we were asked by Breakfast TV to play, 'Summer Holiday' outside Wimbledon on the first day of the tournament with Darren Day singing at 6.30am in the morning to those who had queued all night. TV companies do this kind of bizarre thing to you but those queuing seemed happy enough though.

Hugh Grant was another big celebrity we'd met. He was with Liz Hurley after a Wembley game in what was known as the, sponsors' village, where all the sponsors would get together after the game and for a couple of games they asked us to play for them which we didn't mind because getting out of the Wembley car park is a nightmare. On the same occasion we bumped into Ulrika Jonsson, who was very pleasant, even exchanging views of the Argentina game at France 98 when we were all in the same end and Ulrika was singing along with the rest of us. Another footballing celebrity that we met at the time was Sam Allardyce at the opening of the National Football Museum in Preston. What you see is what you get with Sam, that came through when we met him.

All of these meetings and happenings were totally crazy but have now become routine, i.e. 'normal'. The difficulty for me is that because bizarre has become 'normal' it is very easy for my mates to take me for a ride. They phone up, suggesting the most off the wall things, knowing that if they successfully disguise their voice they will get me, hook, line and sinker.

Chapter Seventeen

Euro 2000 was over and we'd played the one friendly game against France but it was real competition that we craved. The draw had been made for the qualifying stages of the next World Cup to be played in Japan in 2002 and it had thrown up some interesting clashes. Finland, Albania, Greece and our old rivals Germany had all been drawn in England's qualifying group all of which would be new countries to visit for us. Not only that, we should surely be able to beat Finland, Albania and Greece which would leave two games against Germany who we had just beaten in Euro 2000. The England/Germany games were the ones that stood out as the most critical and they were the ones that we were looking forward to most.

The wait for the first of those games wasn't very long; the home fixture against Germany was announced as the first of the World Cup qualifying campaign, the date being set for 7th October 2000. This date was all the more special when we learned that it would be the last competitive England international to be played under the famous twin towers of Wembley stadium. The famous old stadium that had hosted so many great games, none more so that England's World Cup Final victory over Germany in 1966, was to be demolished and a new state of the art stadium built in its place. The new stadium was promised to be the best football stadium in the world.

The game itself was very important. If you are going to qualify for any major tournament you need to win your home games and grab whatever points you can when away from home. The crowd were up for the game and so were we in the band. Everyone wanted the fairy-tale ending to Wembley stadium's hosting of so many famous footballing moments, everyone except the German's of course.

The atmosphere at the start of the game was electric with verbal taunting going on from both sets of fans. The German fans enjoy singing to us in English usually, 'Football's coming home' and they were in full voice. We're very conscious at these games of not taking the banter too far so songs like the Dam busters tune, Dad's Army theme and others about Hitler are deemed a bridge too far for any game, never mind this one. The Great Escape however is a tune that we always play and it was booming out.

Kevin Keegan had a fully fit squad to choose from before kick-off which so often happens when the game is one that matters. On such occasions many players gain miraculous recoveries from whatever injuries they have. We were determined to make the most of our last appearance at the old Wembley too and didn't stop once the game got under way. That was until Liverpool's Hamann scored for Germany from a thirty yard free kick on fourteen minutes.

The goal seemed to knock the stuffing out of us and the crowd. This wasn't how the script was written. We'd beaten Germany only a few months earlier, we should have beaten them in Euro 96 here at Wembley and it was the last game at the stadium - they couldn't come here and win!

The band will never lie down no matter what and at one nil there's plenty of hope. We will always give everything for ninety minutes and fans look to us to do that to inspire noise from the terraces, so, after a few words of encouragement down the line and amongst fans around us we got going again. Murray is usually first on the drum with der, der, der der der, der der derd der England! After this we're at it full pelt but try as we might the game remained a lack-lustre affair with relatively few chances for England and those that we had we didn't convert. There was a bit of decent creeping in from the crowd towards the team as we looked like losing to our arch rivals.

England did lose and at the end of the game there was a mixed reaction with some fans booing and in particular as Kevin Keegan left the field to go down the tunnel behind the goal at our end we could see some fans having a go at him. This we thought was a bit over the top but that's football when emotions run high and the team have lost, rightly or wrongly, the fans often have a go.

We thought no more of the incident and, disappointed though we were, we hung around a little longer after the final whistle than we normally would to have a last look at the old stadium. We weren't on our own, with little pockets of fans remaining in their seats, taking time to reflect on their memories, almost as if they were in prayer in church pews rather than in a football stadium. It was a sad time for many, including us. Wembley had become another home for us and it was going to disappear. It was where we made our debut on the international stage four years earlier as a group of very nervous individuals and where we'd developed a bond with the fans and team that hadn't happened before and it was to be no more.

All the members of the band had given a lot and made massive commitments to play for England at Wembley taking time from work, or in my case from my business; not that we were complaining as we regard it as an honour to be able to do what we do. Personal relationships had suffered too, as they do with many dedicated football fans when it comes to football versus home life. Would we change it? Not a prayer but the moment at the end of the game got to many of us that night.

"Come on lads", said a steward when the time came to move on and we left the stadium for the last time.

Finding your car in the Wembley car park is a real task after a match although it does improve with experience. As we walked through the cars and crowd we sensed a bit of a buzz. People were listening intently to their radios. We jumped into the car and tuned in to Radio 5 to hear that Kevin Keegan had resigned as England manager straight after the game. The report was that he didn't think he was tactically aware enough to manage at international level. That may be so but we couldn't help thinking, knowing that Keegan was a man who wore his heart on his sleeve, that the fans having a go at him at the tunnel end of Wembley as he left the field that night, had pushed him over the edge. We were really disappointed to hear the news. We'd shared the highs and lows together over the last year including Euro 2000 and really appreciated the praise Kevin had given us and the fans during our time together, particularly after the Charleroi games.

That was that, the end of an era, on one, two or even three fronts our last visit to Wembley as we knew it, the end of the Keegan era and the last appearance of the band at the old Wembley for a while. Or so we thought.

There was one more twist to the tale. Sky Sports phoned us up the following day to ask if we could come down to Wembley again later that week to witness the beginning of the demolition of the stadium and the twin towers. There was a function on at the same time that we were there in a marquee next to the stadium to commemorate everything that was great and good about Wembley stadium. The great and good of football were gathered there for the function and we didn't mean to upset anything when we started playing on Sky's instruction but our start up tune coincided with the speeches inside the marquee prompting an official to sprint out towards us to quieten us down. We did so very apologetically and waited for the function to finish before we did our bit.

The demolition crane was ready next to the famous twin towers with the concrete ball swinging in preparation for the first strike. The world's press had turned out to watch the event when they asked us to play a tune. There was only one tune that could be played on such an occasion so after a drum roll I put the trumpet to my lips and played 'The Last Post' as best I could to the complete respect of all around us.

The England Band were now established and ready to go on tour with England around the different grounds at home as well as abroad during the building of the new Wembley stadium. For a moment though this was a time of reflection, The Last Post was the first tune I'd learnt as a seven year old cub scout in Sheffield all those years ago.

Who knew what lay in store for us next, if the past was anything to go by there wasn't much chance of predicting it, laughs apart, other than to say that together with the England fans we'll be giving every last ounce of energy and passion that we have to encourage the team to victory, wherever we are.

Chapter Eighteen

Who are ya? by Stephen Holmes

Since 1993 we have had many band members, who have, 'dipped their toe in,' been mainstays of the band or done, 'one off appearances.'

The single thing that has united every person who has been a band member was their desire to help their club and country and to help increase the atmosphere at each game we have played.

The ability of each person who has been in the band to play their instrument.....can only be explained as, 'amazingly awesome.......to absolutely useless!'

In the following paragraphs I'll attempt to introduce each of the people who have stood behind the brass or banged the drum......despite their ability......they have achieved the goal of, 'playing for England.'

Every one of the people mentioned have at some point helped the band, and we thank them for their help. Over the years we have all made some great friends, friendships that will be with us for life, a special group of people who have made for many years, a unique noise!

My big worry is that I can't write my own profile so.....I'll just have to take what comes on the chin...(Or chins!)

Muz

The Brass
John Hemmingham - Band Leader and Trumpet
Nickname – 'Emma'
1993 - Present
England Appearances - 150 +

'It all started with a bugle at Everton'....if I had a pound for every time I'd stood next to John and listened to how the band started!

John is the band leader, I'm not really sure what to say about John – he usually has enough to say about himself.

He is a different class, a great friend.....but at times he gets right on my nerves....We clash more times in a day than you could imagine......but, as he says in broad

Yorkshire, "It'll be oreeeight," (translated to: "stop worrying old bean....it will all be OK!")

He did, for a number of years, believe he had blonde hair! And we're not convinced he doesn't use eye liner!

Firey, passionate & driven - quite simply he has been the driving force behind the band since he formed it in 1993. His proudest moment was when he received the call from Glenn Hoddle; I've never seen him as proud as he was that day. He cares passionately about each band member – even though at times they wouldn't know it.

A bigger Sheffield Wednesday fan, you will struggle to find!

He blows the trumpet louder than I've ever heard....I'm sure that has been a contributing factor to his lesser known nickname of, 'hemmaroyds.'

I have been his room mate, for over 15 years....there's not a lot I don't know about him.....I'll ensure that lot gets to print if I survive him!

I was honoured to be his best man at his marriage to his wife, Jayne, I probably have more arguments with him than any other person in the world......but that's just the way it is.

Emma, "You did it your way.....and did everything!"

Laurence Garratty- Trumpet
Nickname – 'Los'
1993 - Present
England Appearances 130+

Los, he was my first boss at work, and as a nervous 17 year old Los interviewed me and gave me my first job.....he is a top man.

When I first met Los, he too had a full head of hair, 'mullet perm' and half his marbles....now he has no hair and none of his marbles......the band has had a wonderful positive impact on his well being!

Good times were had with Los in the early 90's while watching our beloved Sheffield Wednesday.

He has a sense of humour like no other in the world, (that is a compliment). I know this to be true because he has shown his unique humour in at least four of the world's continents and not one person out of the 1,000's we have met have ever 'got him.'

Quite simply, a legend, he's deep...as deep as deep can be but a comedy genius...bordering on madness!

A great Dad to his daughter, Rowen, Los has managed to balance his family life with Jules and running a business very well with his commitment to his best mates in the band.

A great friend, who will always make time for you.

Los is a very good musician; he plays the Great Escape in his own unique way, a way that no other musician in the world could play it!

Los takes a great picture, he has the knack of being able to steal the show in any photograph we have taken, his timing and delivery of a one liner or a grimace is simply, World Class.....Los – The David Beckham of the one liner!

Los, "You're just too good to be true!"

Steve Wood - Euphonium
Nickname – (or in Ken's case real name) - Ken Barlow
1995 - Present
England Apperances -120 +

Right then Ken...

Ken's a teacher....he is also many other things to many other people...but we'll leave that for another day.

A band legend, Ken has helped our band so much over the years with unbelievable personal sacrifices, and although we never say thanks....he means the world to us - we just wouldn't be the same without him.

It will come as no surprise; Ken used to be a match day steward to Sheffield Wednesday, and gave up his role to join us on the Kop!

A good family man, who has 2 children, again he does wonderfully well to balance band duties and keeping Katie (his wife) and Rosie & Tom, (his children) happy.

Ken is our number one target for wind-up's.....for a very well educated man, he is so gullible!

Ken is an awesome Euphonium player who plays so loud, the band just isn't the same when he's not able to make a game.

During his time with the band, he has been a Veggie, a Vegan...you name it he's been it. He has also had so many different conditions - that no one else has ever heard of!

Despite his 'eating fads' it has never stopped him eating a full English breakfast every time we go away!

Ken's humour is a little bit 'off the wall.' He often sits in a corner giggling to himself....and never shares the joke.....this then leads to a barrage of rubber bands making their way to his now, bald head!

"Der der der der Ken's a Teacher!"

Christopher Hancock- Euphonium
Nickname - Hanky
2001 - to Present
England Apperances - 75 +

Hanky, what can I say?

214

He came to audition at the Sheffield Wednesday open day, he brought all his family along, he was a little ginger kid from 'Rovram' (Rotherham to those not from 'Rovrum'), he'd played in the local Salvation Army Band and his dream was to play with the Sheffield Wednesday Kop band!

I guess he would have been about 14 when he joined us, and we've seen him 'grow' into a young man.

Hanky takes a great picture which is fortunate because he's not so good with the spoken word!

He's got a great family around him who are very proud of their little star!

Hanky had not been out of South Yorkshire before he joined the band - he's now been across the globe stretching from Japan to Las Vegas!

He's matured into a great lad, with a blossoming sense of humour, a massive Sheffield Wednesday fan, who also enjoys the odd game of rugby!

We are so proud of Hanky and treat him as a family member, we literary would do anything for him; he is a top man....who we all 'love' dearly!

He's not a lover of 'good' food; and much prefers fast food in particular one major brand!

He always finishes his meals with a bag of F***ing Hot Monster Munch! (Don't deny it, you all do it!)

He is a legend in the band for his insane 'one liners' completely unaware he's even said half of them!

We're hoping that one day he'll find someone 'special' and settle down.... What a wedding that would be!

It might happen by the time he's 40! (15 years to go then) - now that would make a good film!

Hanky....is simply Hanky to us!

Luke Modiri - Trumpet
Nickname – Shabba
2004 - To Present
England Appearances - 50 +

Shabba joined the band as a young man who was studying for his GCSE's......many years on he's at University, still studying!

It just goes to show what a positive influence we have been on his education, with constant support from every band member!

Shabs is a great guy (if a little moody at times!); he is a very good trumpet player, who can play very loud and is a huge asset to the band.

Shabs is a caring and thoughtful young man who has a great family who give him a great deal of support and have given him a great start in life! (He's a lucky lad!)

Shabs, like Hanky, is a huge Wednesday fan, and loves watching football.

He particularly appreciates Loz helping him with his course work especially with illustrations!

Shabba has been on many trips with us, and often rooms with his best mate - Hanky, they really have 'hit it off.'

Shabba, is now almost married to Rach (from Rochdale) – we can't wait to see Shabba's next steps in life.....the big question is, will he join the family firm (Modiri....& Son) or will he go it alone?

Our proudest 'Shabba moment' was being invited to his 18th birthday party.....as usual we were very reserved and gave a good impression of ourselves to shabba's many friends and family.

Shabbs doesn't like waiting, is a tad impatient and can have quite a short fuse......but in spite of this he has never ever lost his temper or stormed off in a huff....never ever!

'Mr Lover man.....Shabba!'

Bram Denton – Saxophone
Nickname - 'Empla Blam'
1995 - to Present
England Appearances - 70 +

Bram is our Emperor; we worship the ground he walks upon.

A retired bank manager and naval officer, Bram amazes us with his great wit and compelling personality.

Barbara, his devoted wife, is quite simply the luckiest woman in the world!

Bram is a wonderful family man, who takes great care of all his family, he loves to spend time with them, and we thank his family from the bottom of our hearts for allowing us to pinch some of their quality time!

Bram, our elder statesman, has kept us on the straight and narrow, he enjoys our humour (most of the time), he has an amazing knowledge which he freely passes on to us younger ones.

Bram has only failed in one thing ....Hanky's elocution lessons, despite many hours of investment in Hanky's grasp of the wonderful English language, Bram gave it up as a bad job; Hanky was simply a lost cause!

I'm sure I speak for every band member who has had the pleasure of Empla Blam's company over the years - you are a legend, and we are all the better for knowing such a great man.

Despite a few, 'senior moments,' Bram has managed to travel the world with us with no major incidents. Bram decided to take a back seat on the travelling around the world and enjoy his time in the garden (even if that includes falling off the Conifers he's cutting!) as well as spending quality time with his Grandson, Rory. He still is a regular fixture with the band at the Wednesday home games, and with some kind Kick-off times makes the line up at Wembley too.

Bram 'there'll always be an England' Denton

Bernie Clifton - Trombone!
Nickname - Bern, Uncle Bern, Bernie Cliff-Top or Rod Hull
2006 - To Present
England appearances - 25 +

National treasure Bern doesn't need any introduction, yes, he's the man on the duck. No.... he didn't fall off his roof when mending his TV aerial.....but yes, he is a true comedy legend.

Bern is a genius, we are so fortunate to have had the pleasure of spending so much quality time with a true British entertainment legend.

But like most genius' there's a fine line between genius and madness....Bern walks this tightrope daily!

Bern offers the band so much, he is just naturally funny. His expressions, his amazing sense of timing...Bern has me in stitches many times a day. I'm sure he won't mind me making this public, but he isn't that good on the Trombone!

Amazingly he lets us help out during his Panto shows.....Oh yes he does! (Although, Hanky now has a lifetime ban from appearing in Panto!)

I first met Bern when he interviewed me on his Radio Sheffield afternoon show, he 'played' his Trombone – John gave him a call and the rest is history. Bern makes time for everyone, and is always the first to ask how my family are & what the boys are up to.

Bern is now a permanent fixture both home and away at England's games.

Bern is keen to ensure old age doesn't catch up and takes great delight in videoing us for around 22 hours of every day; he doesn't miss a trick and sets most of the tricks up without us even knowing!

Bern and Los are soul-mates: a great friendship with one thing in common.....they are both barking mad!

The simplest of tasks...like ordering Sausage and Chips at a service station becomes a rib tickling half hour orgy of pure laughter – Bern is a true gent, who has given so many laughs to so many people over a great career and now we're so lucky to have a front row ticket every day of the week.

"Is it a bird....is it a plane....no it's a man on a duck.....der der der der Bernie Clifftop!"

Alistair Dyson - Euphonium
Nickname - 'AL' - not a very interesting
nickname.....but it is what it is!
2000 To Present
England Appearances - 60 +

Al is a very thoughtful and clearly intelligent guy.

He loves to sit back and watch an unsuspecting band member fall into one of our set-up's - a crime that is almost as bad as the set up itself.

A quiet guy, who is a very good musician, a big Wednesdayite, Al was introduced to the band by Ken, who met him while playing for the Stannington Brass Band (a band that can actually play and read music!)

Al took some time to 'get us' but now he's had years of practice and can read us like a book....I know he cringes whenever we are in a Restaurant, I know he wishes we were not so boisterous....but we are!

Al seems to like taking a shower in his car; he never closes the windows or locks his doors, and inevitably this means he'll have a car bath.....I've lost count of the number of times Al has allowed his car to become a bathing vehicle!

Al now lives in Hull with his long-term girlfriend - he is a valuable member of the band who has been very loyal to the cause.

An interesting fact about Al is that he researches the scents that go into our household cleaning products!

Big 'AL'......Big 'AL'......Big 'AL'

Alex Dunhill - Trumpet
Nickname - 'Lix'
2000 - Present
England Appearances - 75 +

Lix is a very likeable young man, now living in Bristol with the love of his life, Jen. Hopefully he'll see the light and move back 'Home' to the North (with Jen)!

Lix is possibly the cleverest person to ever come out of Maltby!

He has a very strange taste in music, and can't half belt out a tune from his instrument. He has been a fantastic servant to the band over a number of years, he'll always help us out when asked.

He loves to travel, and loved his time in Vegas with us; I've never seen anybody as enthused about a piece of rock as he was in the Grand Canyon!

Lix is also a big Wednesdayite, who loves a good discussion - he's quite easy to wind up, and sometimes struggles to spot a wind-up until it's too late!

Again, a good sense of humour and a very grounded young man who knows exactly what he wants from life.....and he'll get it!

He loves an argument with John.....and more often than not a trip includes one!

I'm sure he styles himself on Ken, he always seems to be one step behind in the fashion stakes.... (NOT).

Lix 'too cool for school' Dunhill

Simon Grayson
Nickname - Adolf
1994 - 2004
2009 - present
England apperances - 60 +

Adolf is an ex pro footballer, who graced the shirts of Hartlepool and Sheffield United (shhhhh) to name a couple of his teams.

Named Adolf because of his renowned German-like efficiency and time-keeping, he is simply far too organised for his own good.

Adolf took a few years out from band duties when his two boys Arnie and Charlie were born, he also decided to build from scratch, with his wife Denise, their new family home. Now settled in his new home and with Arnie and Charlie growing up Adolf is back with us.

He plays the Trumpet as loud as John, but the after effects via bottom burping are a high price to pay for the extra volume.

Adolf has a very dry sense of humour (amazing there is any humour considering we think he's German!) He loves a wind up and is always very cautious to ensure he's never the butt of a joke or wind up....unfortunately he's been caught a few times.....don't mention the toothpick!

It's good to have Adolf back with us, I've really missed his company....let's hope they stop at two kids!

Simon 'what F***ing time do you call this' Grayson

Our most recent recruits have joined us over the past 2 years or so, and are just beginning to make their mark on the band......and us on them! The following are a permanent fixture in our Wembley home games:

James Shelton - joined us in 2006, lives in Norwich and is a big Wednesday fan; he fulfilled an ambition when he joined us on the Kop playing at Hillsborough, an ever present at Wembley since he joined the band.

James plays the trumpet (very well) and works for the Norfolk FA; he's hoping to continue his studies in Sheffield, where I'm sure we'll see a lot more of him!

Piers Shelton - James's younger brother joined us in 2008, also a very good trumpet player. Piers has become a regular feature in the Wembley line-up. His favourite moment was the Croatia 5-1 by England at Wembley.

Julian - Trombone, a happy hammer! Julian is London based, he is studying something very complicated and is a very likeable young man, and he loves his football and following England.

He shies away from any limelight and simply loves watching the beautiful game.

Campbell Freeman - one of our Salvation Army recruits, a very talented musician, who is a great bloke, is always on hand to help us out and is an ever present at Wembley. Campbell takes a great picture and is often seen holding a classic model pose! Campbell's bravest move was to introduce his daughter to Hanky......luckily for Campbell the only sweet music played that night was the Great Escape!

Mark Sefton - like Campbell, Mark is another Salvation Army recruit. He's a very talented and likeable guy, who plays trombone, again he is becoming a mainstay of the Wembley line up. He loves his fish and chips......but not the price! Mark is the architect of many a rubber band war! A Proper dark horse!

Nigel Wood - Finishes a hat-trick of recruits from the Salvation Army. Nigel introduced us to Campbell and Mark, an excellent trumpet player and a very keen football man who is heavily involved in grassroots football in his home town Scarborough. Nigel also owns his own IFA practice.

That finishes our current line up of Brass..... We have of course had many other brass players who no longer join the line up:

Ian Bamford - A recruit from Stannington band, and Wednesdayite, Ian has been unable to play with us since 2008 due to his work commitments. Ian has played his trombone many times for England, both home and away for around 8 years, he really came into his own in Las Vegas, where he lived the dream! Ian is a top man who is sorely missed and is always welcome to join us. Ian is a good mate and an all round good bloke.

Julie Heliwell - Jules, our 1st female band member! How she put up with us for the number years she did.... I really don't know! She deserves a medal.

Jules travelled to England and Wednesday games from her home in Driffield, North Yorkshire. She showed tremendous dedication, and is a great person.

Jules' career meant that the band had to take a back seat, but her presence over the years has been invaluable in the band growing as it did. Thanks Jules for putting up with us and for all you did for the band.

Brian Towse - 'Cast' is a huge Wednesday fan, with his wife, Barbara. Brian is a professional musician, who couldn't quite work how we actually got on!

His love of pizza dominated our trips away, as did his enjoyment of having breakfast with the band.

'Cast' had an answer-phone message the Queen would have been proud of..... sooo posh!

Cast brought along his son, Kelvin, to play with the band on a number of occasions.

From my recollections his favourite band was 90's group, Prodigy, he even styled his hair on them, and he really was a fire- starter!

Brian is quite simply the most talented trumpet player I have ever heard - a pizza eating music legend!

We miss you 'Cast'.....no, honestly, we really do!

Sarah Hancock – 'Scary'

Scary is Hanky's younger sister, she plays the trumpet and keeps Chris 'in check'!

Sarah has spent many hours travelling up and down the country to games biting her lip – for 90% of the journey time!

Sarah plays the trumpet, very well and very loud.....but once she found romance....the band came second best.

She keeps promising to make a guest appearance, if only to give her brother a lift to the ground!

The Hancock dynasty continues......with Chris and Sarah in Tandem the sky is the limit!

Other guests include two of Adolf's cousins who live in Southampton and helped us out in the early days,

Helen Chamberlain (of Soccer AM fame) and Radio One presenter, 'Jamie Student bloke.'

Well that's the Brass covered.....a big thanks to everyone who has helped us out over the years.....now for the real talent.....the very musical Drummers!

The Drummers

It's either something I've said or the fact that my rhythm is so poor they leave because I'm a lost cause......the latter is more likely to be true.

The following introductions are of the many drumming partners I have had over the past 17 years or so.

I have had the pleasure to drum with every one of the these guys, we really have made one hell of a racket over the years and played during games for thousands of hours, the partners come and go but he drum beat stays the same....

I'll leave it to John to do my profile, but would just like to thank each and every one of the band from the bottom of my heart for the friendships and laughs I have had since we started the band.

Quite simply, I have had the time of my life, I always wear my heart on my sleeve and have loved every single minute of the past 17 years....and can't wait for the next 17 years!

I'm immensely proud of what we do and have done, and have a great passion for our Country and making it proud. I'll just finish and get on with the introductions with a thankyou to my wonderful wife, Fiona, and our boys, Adam and Richard, for putting up with my long-term absences....! Your support is amazing - Love Ya X

Right then 'The Drummers....'

Stephen Holmes – Drummer and Band Director
Nickname – Murray, Muz, Muzworker
1993 – present
England appearances 150+

(Stephen Holmes profile by John Hemmingham)

Murray has been there from the start of the band in 1993 and shared all the moments since. Before he started in the band he'd never banged a drum in his life but boy can he bang it now!

He's got the essential combination of football watching experience and passion that are so important to the band. He knows when to start, when to stop and when to keep going and supplies the effort and enthusiasm to be the heartbeat of the band.

When we started in 1993 Murray had a full head of hair and was maybe three stones lighter than he is now. He's sacrificed a lot for the band, including one of his lungs when it collapsed whilst playing, and he ended up in hospital having it inflated again. He has a loyalty to the band second-to-none.

He is a massive Sheffield Wednesday fan, not missing games at home for years and doing a stint of thirteen years without missing away too. England is a particular passion of his, he kick's every ball.

We room together all over the world and often lie in bed at the end of the day, wherever we are, and after a long exhalation he may say, 'This is ******* ridiculous!' We can often be found shouting at each other on the terrace because our passions have overflowed.

He is happily married to Fiona, with grown up boys, Adam and Richard, and couldn't have a happier home life.

He's also enjoying having some success doing his bit as a coach in local football, which is a passion of his.

If ever there was a need, Murray would be there for me, as I would be for him, which is simply invaluable. Top man.

Joe Herridge
Nickname 'Juha'
1996 - Present (with a few gaps when he went AWOL)
England Apperances - 60 +

Joe is a fantastic fella, we've watched him grow up from an aspiring young schoolboy who wanted to rule the world, to a traveller who wanted to get the world tattooed on his body, who is now a hard working, fine young man who'll be one hell of an architect (when he finally qualifies).

Joe has a great family, who support him more than he will ever know!

He's a great drummer who has got so much enthusiasm for everything he does.

Joe is what the band is all about..... He loves a laugh, he loves his football and he has grown with the band over the years.

I know he cringes at our pranks, jokes & wind up's....he pretends that he hasn't seen or heard them, but his smile is infectious and he can't contain his laughter!

Joe has had many 'run-in's' with John, especially when he was a moody, spotty adolescent who knew best. He used to throw a great teenage tantrum, unfortunately. John was a master of encouraging a repeat performance....Joe, as usual, never let us down and delivered!

Joe will be a friend for life....and he knows we will always be there for him.

Johnny Hayward
Nickname - Johnny Boy
2006 - present
England Appearances - 25 +

Johnny is a free spirit, you never know where he'll be when you ring him.

He loves to travel, and he loves his football.

His best mate in the band is Shabba, they have got so much in common!

He's got a very strange West Yorkshire accent, and a very strange desire to live in obscure countries, he's lived in China, Vietnam and South Africa in the past 18 months!

I think that Johnny is unique in that for the first time in 17 years I'm actually better than someone, he has a strange drumming style, and his facial expressions are very odd!

He's learning how to deal with us, but it has been a very large learning curve.

He's also just learning how far he can go with us, in the wind-up stakes..... He often over-steps the mark, only to be put in his place rather abruptly!

Johnny has got a great heart, he never shuts up, he never sleeps, he never returns your calls, he never returns your texts.....but he's got a great passion....so there's always a place for Johnny!

Johnny 'where the F**K are you' Hayward

Johnny Corcoran
Nickname 'Johnny the Rhino'
2001- Present (2007 England Band)
England Appearances – 15 +

Johnny the rhino, Johnny, is a weightlifter.....no really he is a weightlifter, and one hell of a snare drummer.

Johnny is so talented on the drums, he really helps us out with his wonderful technique.

Johnny is quite a laid back young man, who just gets on with the task in hand without any fuss.

He's called Johnny the Rhino because he is 'JOHNNY THE RHINO' - Simple!

I'm sure there is lot more to come from Johnny over the coming years, he's a bit of a dark horse, who I'm sure will give us a few surprises as time goes on.

So that's the current crop of drummers, now I'll introduce the guys who have drummed for England over the past 17 years.

I wish I knew everyone's real name.....but its nicknames only I'm afraid.

Stephen Shooter
Nickname - 'SHOOTER'
2003 - 2007
England Appearances – 20 +

Shooter is a legend, he joined the band as a jack the lad, larger than life 14-15 year old, who could hit the drum so hard it was unbelievable.

By the time he left the band to concentrate on looking after his family, he was 6ft tall, and looked hard as nails......but underneath, as Philippa, (Shooters other half) will agree, he's a big softy.

Shooter is a huge Wednesday fan, who loves his football.

I remember Shooter being blown away with the celebrities at the Soccer Aid after show party at Old Trafford, with Zola, Maradona, Dunga, Robbie Williams and many more - but the photo he really wanted was Fizz from Coronation St!

We still hope that Shooter will come back into the fold and get back on board with us - open invite Shooter!

SHOOOOOOOOOOOOTERRRRRR!

Ben Senior
Nickname - 'BEN' very original!
2003 - 2007
England Appearances – 15 +

Ben and his Dad (Mick) are devoted Owls. Ben is a very talented Drummer who is now working behind the camera – filming all the Sheffield Wednesday games, while he completes his studies, a very focused young man, who is a great lad.

Very passionate about his football and loves the positive impact that a good atmosphere can have on the players.

Jimmy
Nickname 'Jimmy'
1994 - 1999
England Appearances - 20 +

Jimmy is a rockstar! My lasting memory of Jim is his long ginger hair and his amazing drumming at the World cup in France, Jimmy is an awesome drummer.

I used to watch in complete awe and amazement at what he could do with a marching drum, a great lad, who decided (sadly) that the band wasn't for him and pursued his chances with his indie band, 'Bhuna.'

Jimmy still goes to the Wednesday matches, and works at Sheffield University, he still keeps in touch. And, more importantly, he's still chasing the dream!

Max Patrick
Nickname - 'Max'
1997 - 2002
England Appearances - 40 +

We've had some very talented drummers in the band over the years, but Max is quite simply the best, so talented, and so passionate, Max for me is a drumming genius.

Max went to live in Milan after the 2002 World Cup, where he got a job as a music teacher. Both he and Mandy, his wife, settled very quickly into the Italian way of life and are still living in Milan with there two children, Benny and Sammy.

Max is now teaching for his day job, writing and performing music, and has the best part time job ever; he's the on-site commentator for the global distribution of Serie 'A' games, mainly AC & Inter Milan!

I'll never forget Max's wonderful snare drumming that introduced the Great Escape in Rome '97, what a special night, made even more special by great drumming from Max.

The following have had fleeting roles in the drumming in the band:

Joe Strummer - Little Joe never really got to grips with our humour, but a good lad and a very good drummer. He always seemed to be underdressed, and he was always strumming something!

Rob 'flob–a-dib' – Rob from Loughborough, a big Wednesdayite who was with us for a couple of years, then University took him away...sadly we've lost touch- A very nice fella.

Jamie - A young man from Hillsborough who sat in front of the band for years and decided to give it a whirl....we're convinced he's still got one of our drums, so maybe he'll either join up again or return the drum?

Lewis Stokes - A right cheeky chappy who certainly could play the snare drum, and was a great laugh, he moved on and we still see him at matches.

Martin Stenton - 'Tino' tried and failed during France '98.....oh dear!

Alan Tootle - tried one game and had an amazing knack of being able to echo every beat I did! Cheers Al!

Michael Denton - One of the original members of the band who left the band sometime after France '98?

Ian - Michael Denton's mate who played the very first match in 1993 and left shortly after because of 'artistic differences!'

Craig Zelly- Zelwar played the first few games and then left!

Steeper and Deadly Darren, Adolf's mate from work who played a couple of games at Wembley, the last time I saw them they were scantily dressed.....at a fancy dress party!

Well, I guess that's it.....If I've left anyone out.....Sorry!

Other non-fiction titles from Peak Publish:

I Hate Football: A Fan's Memoir by John Firth
ISBN: 978-1-907219-02-3

Coaldust to Stardust by Jackie Toaduff
ISBN: 978-1-907219- 08-5 (Hbk)
ISBN: 978-1-907219 -14-6 (Pbk)

Best of France: 8 Favourite Themed Tours
by Trevor Snow
ISBN: 978-1-907219- 06-1

344 A Story of the Pretoria Pit Disaster: Inspired
by a Mother's Tale by Andrea Jane Finney
ISBN: 978-1-907219-00-9

Goodbye Old Chap: A Life at Sea in Peace and
War by Philip Algar
ISBN: 978-1-907219- 04-7

No Retreat by Chris F Coley
ISBN: 978-1-907219-05-4

The Railway Revolution: Railways and their
Impact on England, 1801-1900 by Paul McDonald
ISBN:978-1-907219-16-0

India Calls: True Call Centre Stories
by Sudhindra Mokhasi
ISBN: 978-1-907219-01-6